Praise for
The Zen Teaching of Homeless Kodo

"Shohaku Okumura is a true treasure for contemporary American Zen, humbly but clearly expressing this noble legacy."
—Taigen Dan Leighton, author of *Zen Questions*

"Sawaki Roshi's profound and simple Dharma expression comes from the depth of his empty, open heart, like the light of the sun or the flow of a river, pure and unhindered, touching and awakening that same place in ourselves."
—Mel Weitsman, founder of Berkeley Zen Center

"Clear and conversational. The variety among the three voices encourages the emergence of a fourth: yours, as you browse and come back again and again."
—Jisho Warner, founder of Stone Creek Zen Center

"Studying this book is a rare chance to sit with three Zen masters as they bring forth the Dharma with their unique family style—compassionate, blunt, humorous, wholehearted—each one devotedly helping the other and helping us to wake up."
—Eijun Linda Ruth Cutts, Central Abbess of the San Francisco Zen Center

The Zen Teaching of Homeless Kodo

Kodo Sawaki

Kosho Uchiyama

Shohaku Okumura

The Zen

TEACHING OF
Homeless Kodo

by Kosho Uchiyama Roshi

Translation and Commentary by
Shohaku Okumura

Edited by
Jokei Molly Delight Whitehead

Wisdom

Wisdom Publications
199 Elm Street
Somerville, MA 02144 USA
wisdomexperience.org

Library of Congress Cataloging-in-Publication Data
Uchiyama, Kosho, 1912–1998 author.
   The Zen teaching of Homeless Kodo / by Kosho Uchiyama Roshi ; Translation and Commentary by Shohaku Okumura ; Edited by Jokei Molly Delight Whitehead.
      pages cm
   Previously published: 1990.
   Includes bibliographical references and index.
   Includes translation from Japanese.
   ISBN 978-1-61429-048-3 — ISBN 1-61429-048-2 (pbk. : alk. paper) — ISBN 978-1-61429-047-6
   1. Sawaki, Kodo, 1880–1965—Teachings. 2. Spiritual life—Zen Buddhism. 3. Monastic and religious life (Buddhism)—Japan. I. Okumura, Shohaku, 1948– II. Title.
   BQ9288.U33 2014
   294.3′4—dc23
                                    2014007279

ISBN 978-1-61429-048-3   ebook ISBN 978-1-61429-047-6

25 24 23 22 21
7 6 5 4 3

The sumi-e portraits of Sawaki Roshi, Uchiyama Roshi, and Shohaku Okumura are courtesy of Michael Hofmann, http://michaeldhofmann.com.
Cover and interior design by Gopa & Ted2, Inc. Set in Palatino LT Standard 10/14.

Printed in the United States of America.

Please visit fscus.org.

This new translation is humbly dedicated to

Somon Kodo Daiosho

on the occasion of the fiftieth anniversary
of his passing away

and

Doyu Kosho Daiosho

on the occasion of the seventeenth
anniversary of his passing away.
Without their teachings and examples,
I could not have found a positive and
creative way of life.

Nine prostrations,
Shohaku Okumura

Contents

The Zen Teaching of Homeless Kodo

Preface
by Jokei Molly Delight Whitehead

There may be no better example of a reckless vow than promising to edit a book. No matter how many times one reads a manuscript with the precise attention that's a kind of love, mistakes will escape. I'd like to say perfection isn't the goal, but perfection has to be the goal, never mind its impossibility. This paradox lends our vows their bittersweet beauty: we strive wholeheartedly for ideals we know we can never reach, accepting failure more or less gracefully from the start.

Here my mission was to help the Dharma express itself as clearly and meaningfully as possible through three generations of a Zen lineage. My favorite aspect of this book is its prismatic reflection of a single truth through the distinct characters, experiences, and voices of three teachers—the universal manifesting through the particular, as always.

I'm honored to have been part of this effort, which gave me a tangible way to express my gratitude to my teacher, Shohaku Okumura, and to our lineage. Across divides of culture and time, I feel a resonance with Kodo Sawaki Roshi, most of all because of his "homelessness"— his skepticism of institutions, religious and otherwise. I believe that for Sawaki Roshi spiritual practice had nothing to do with signing on to a particular dogma, but instead meant shouldering responsibility moment by moment for the truth and vitality of one's own life, intimate with all things.

Along with devotion and responsibility, life asks trust—trust in what Dogen Zenji called "total function." In the end, an editor has to trust the words themselves, the truth behind them, and the earnest intentions of readers, then take a deep breath and let the book have its life. May you enjoy it!

xiv | the zen teaching of homeless kodo

My thanks to those who kept me on path at the beginning of my practice: Leslie James, Diana Gerard, and Norma Fogelberg. To Christopher Stillson for his unwavering faith and generosity of spirit. And to the friends who fed and sheltered me in my "homeless" days as a priest in Bloomington, Indiana: Peiwei Li and Arjan Vermeulen, Alexis Wreden and Robert Fakelmann, Barbara Moss and Bob Meadows, Beth and Tom Hollingsworth, Brian Flaherty, and Yuko Okumura.

I dedicate my work here to my parents, Joan and Jeff Whitehead, who taught me to love words—the right ones, in the right order, and not too many of them.

Introduction
by Shohaku Okumura

This book is a collection of Kosho Uchiyama Roshi's comments on selected short sayings of Kodo Sawaki Roshi. I added some explanation to help contemporary Western readers understand the examples from Japanese history and culture and the essential points of their teachings in a wider Buddhist context.

Sawaki Roshi was one of the most important Soto Zen Buddhist masters of twentieth-century Japan. His fifty years of teaching throughout Japan made Soto Zen available to the common people, outside the traditional monastic system. His emphasis on the traditional sewing of robes has also been widely influential on Western Soto Zen.

Sawaki Roshi's Dharma heir Uchiyama Roshi was a rare Japanese Soto Zen master with a graduate degree in Western philosophy. His unique way of presenting the Dharma appeals to the modern intellect.

The two teachers' complementary personalities, combined with their sense of humor, offer us practical guidance in Zen Buddhism and help readers make sense of the challenges of our modern world.

The History of This Book

The main part of this book, the wisdom from Kodo Sawaki Roshi and commentary by Kosho Uchiyama Roshi, originally appeared as a series of newspaper articles by Uchiyama Roshi, which ran from January 1966 to February 1967 in the religious column of the Japanese newspaper *Asahi Shimbun*. The fifty-six articles were compiled and published by Hakujusha Press as two volumes in 1966 and 1967. For the seventh anniversary of Sawaki Roshi's death, Uchiyama Roshi wrote fifteen additional articles (chapters 57–71 in this book), and all were combined into a pocket-sized volume.

Ten years later, Uchiyama Roshi added his essay "Kodo Sawaki Roshi's Zazen"and republished the book. This piece is based on a talk he gave in 1980 at Jinnoin temple; located in Kure, Hiroshima, Jinnoin is one of the temples Sawaki Roshi visited regularly as part of his "moving monastery."

These early versions were all released by Hakujusha, publisher of the majority of Uchiyama Roshi's books. In the 1990s, Hakujusha folded, and his more than twenty books went out of print.

After Uchiyama Roshi's death, one of his Dharma heirs, Rev. Shusoku Kushiya, added chapter 72 from an article Uchiyama Roshi wrote in 1985 for the Buddhist magazine *Daihorin*, as well as the essay "Recollections of My Teacher, Kodo Sawaki Roshi," which Uchiyama Roshi wrote in 1971. This latest version was published in 2006 by Daihorinkaku press, which has republished several of Uchiyama Roshi's books, thanks to Rev. Kushiya's efforts.

The book you are reading is based on my English translation of this version.

English Translations

Another of Uchiyama Roshi's Dharma heirs, Rev. Koshi Ichida, with assistance from Marshall Mittnick, made the first English translation of the seventy-one original chapters of this book. He used them as teaching material for the sitting group he led at Pioneer Valley Zendo in Charlemont, Massachusetts, in the second half of the 1970s.

In 1989 at Kyoto Soto Zen Center, I translated the essay "Kodo Sawaki Roshi's Zazen." George Varvares and I edited this and Rev. Ichida's work and published them in 1990 through the center as *The Zen Teaching of "Homeless" Kodo*. Later, this volume was republished as a free teaching resource by Sotoshu Shumucho, Tokyo, Japan. This version has been out of print since 2010.

Both Rev. Ichida and George Varvares passed away in the 1990s. I would like to express my deepest gratitude for their work.

In September 2011, I started to work on this new translation of the Daihorinkaku version. I added my commentary on Sawaki Roshi's

Dharma words and Uchiyama Roshi's explanations. I also wrote a brief biography of Sawaki Roshi. My disciple Jokei Molly Whitehead edited this translation and commentary. I deeply appreciate her excellent work. Without her, this book could not have been published this promptly and in this condition.

Sawaki Roshi and Uchiyama Roshi spoke and wrote about their insights into Buddhadharma using their own unique expressions, without many technical terms. They spoke mainly based on their own experiences and used contemporary colloquial Japanese expressions with concrete examples familiar to ordinary Japanese. This is what made their talks and books popular in Japan.

However, non-Japanese readers unfamiliar with Japanese history, culture, and society at that time might have difficulty understanding their essential points. And unless readers are versed in Buddhism and Zen in general, and Dogen Zenji's teachings in particular, they might have trouble understanding these teachings in this larger context. This is why I decided to offer some explanations and comments. I hope these additions are not superfluous, like putting legs on a painting of a snake.

Unless otherwise cited, any translations of other works, for instance excerpts from Dogen Zenji, are by me.

The Significance of This Book in My Life

During summer vacation in 1965, when I was a seventeen-year-old high school student, my classmate Masanori Uda visited Antaiji, where Uchiyama Roshi lived, to practice for about two weeks. This was right after Uchiyama Roshi had published his first book, *Jiko*, or *Self*, and he gave Masanori a copy. After returning from Antaiji, my friend lent me the book. When I first read it, I wanted to live like Uchiyama Roshi and become his disciple. Masanori and I planned to visit Antaiji in the fall for a five-day sesshin, but in the end we couldn't go. Because of this, I lost my chance to meet Sawaki Roshi; he passed away on December 21 of that year. While I regret that I couldn't meet him, I was also fortunate I couldn't go then—if I'd done my first sesshin at seventeen, I'm sure I would have thought I couldn't do zazen.

The following February, Masanori had surgery for stomach pain he'd suffered since the previous fall. He had intestinal cancer. Because he was young, the cancer grew quickly. The surgeon couldn't do anything for him. Masanori died at the end of July. I visited his family occasionally to offer incense to him. Soon afterward, Masanori's mother called on Uchiyama Roshi at Antaiji. When she mentioned her son's death, Uchiyama Roshi put his photo, together with that of a girl who had recently committed suicide, in his Bible. He said to Masanori's mother, "I hope they become friends in heaven."

That was my first experience losing someone close. It was very painful. I knew that his mother must have had much deeper pain and sadness, but I couldn't say anything to console her. Once when I visited, she showed me newspaper clippings of the articles by Uchiyama Roshi that later became the foundation for the chapters of this book. When she talked about the articles, she smiled. It seemed she got solace from them. This experience strengthened my desire to become Uchiyama Roshi's disciple.

After I started studying Buddhism at Komazawa University in 1968, I tried to read Dogen Zenji's writings, but they were too difficult for me. On the other hand, *The Zen Teaching of Homeless Kodo* was very clear, even for a twenty-year-old university student. Until my understanding deepened and I was able to follow the Buddha's and Dogen Zenji's teachings, this book was my guide in seeking the way.

The most important point I learned from it was that both Sawaki Roshi and Uchiyama Roshi were free of the worldly system of values, and yet they were walking in a very clear direction. I was skeptical of the paths recommended by my parents, teachers, and Japanese society, so I couldn't find a life direction that made sense to me. If I hadn't encountered Sawaki Roshi and Uchiyama Roshi, and through them Dogen Zenji and Shakyamuni Buddha, it might not have been possible for me to live my life positively, with unshakable direction.

Because these articles appeared in a major newspaper, not only for Buddhists or Zen practitioners but mainly addressed to ordinary readers, most of them relate to problems modern people experience in their daily lives. I hope this English translation is helpful for people who wish to find a stable way of life and the meaning of Zen practice in this modern world.

Sawaki Roshi's Multifaceted Life and Personality

As Uchiyama Roshi observes in his "Recollections," Sawaki Roshi was a complex and changeable person. Although most of us have many sides, we often make an effort to appear consistent in various aspects of our lives. However, Sawaki Roshi was openly multifaceted. He showed different traits with his disciples at Antaiji, with priest students at Komazawa University and other temples, with lay students, with those who weren't his students, and with the general public. Each person's image of Sawaki Roshi might be quite different.

In chapter 5, Uchiyama Roshi, the closest and longest disciple of Sawaki Roshi, says that for him the core of Sawaki Roshi's greatness was that he was a person who "wasted" his entire life on zazen. This was the side of Sawaki Roshi's life and teachings that Uchiyama Roshi focused on.

When I started to study Dogen Zenji at Komazawa, I read the whole nineteen-volume collection of Sawaki Roshi's lectures, *Sawaki Kodo Zenshu*, which contained several talks on Dogen's *Shobogenzo*. Even though at this time in my life Dogen was beyond my understanding, Sawaki Roshi's commentaries were interesting. I was very much influenced by many of his teachings. But there were some comments I could not accept: those about war.

In his youth, as a soldier, Sawaki Roshi seemed to feel it was a Japanese man's duty to fight for emperor and nation. He was twenty years old at the time of his service and had little formal education. Roshi kept this attitude until the end of World War II, when his opinion seemed to change; in chapter 16, he says that he can see no point to war. While his adoptive father was alive, Sawaki Roshi used his military pension to support him. Afterward, he used this pension to print copies of Buddhist texts, which he offered free to students and practitioners. He said the pension wasn't "clean" money, so he wanted to use it for the sake of Dharma rather than himself.

I was born in 1948, three years after World War II ended. I was educated very differently from Sawaki Roshi and Uchiyama Roshi. Sawaki Roshi's early sayings about war disturbed me. At school I was taught that the Meiji government fabricated a state religion in which the emperor was a god, and forced Japanese people to believe the best fate was to work hard and die in battle for their nation's sake. Eventually the Japanese military invaded other countries, colonized Taiwan and Korea, and caused millions of deaths. After World War II, Japan accepted an American-made constitution, renouncing military power and resolving never to engage in war. This was my generation's understanding of Japan's history from 1868 to 1945.

Although I appreciated his teachings about zazen and *Shobogenzo* and Dogen's other writings, it wasn't possible for me to accept this aspect of Sawaki Roshi. I was uncomfortable when older people praised Sawaki Roshi as a hero of the Russo-Japanese War, and when people boasted of his interactions with military leaders, government officers, and successful businessmen. From that time, I limited my study of Sawaki Roshi. I tried to follow his teachings only from Uchiyama Roshi's perspective—Sawaki Roshi's greatness was due to having "wasted" his life for zazen. I tried not to quote his sayings except those discussed by Uchiyama Roshi. In this book, I've kept this same attitude.

Some people might argue that such a limited description of his life might give readers a distorted image of Sawaki Roshi. In his book *Zen at War*, Brian Victoria quoted several of Sawaki Roshi's wartime sayings and criticized his support of the military government and the imperial system. Victoria also wrote:

> In an attempt to show at least some of the complexity of the Zen Buddhist response to Japan's military actions, I have included sections on Zen Buddhist war resisters as well as collaborators. On whichever side of the fence these Buddhists placed themselves, their motivations were far more complex than can be presented in a single volume. Nor, of course, can their lives and accomplishments be evaluated solely on the basis of their positions regarding the relationship of Zen to the state and warfare. A holistic evaluation of these leaders, however, is not the subject of this book.

Similarly, my book does not evaluate Sawaki Roshi and his life as a whole objectively and critically. Though such a book would be a worthy undertaking, it would be a different work from this one. Uchiyama Roshi focused his original book on the essential Dharma teaching of Sawaki Roshi; I followed this approach.

Recently, I received an email from a friend in Poland:

> The issue of Roshi Sawaki and *Zen at War* came up. I am wondering what you would answer to somebody who says, "Sawaki is dangerous and not a Buddhist master at all. He killed many people with enthusiasm and didn't feel any remorse, not to mention repentance. His actions during WWII were shameful. That's enough about compassion and true practice of Dharma . . . ."

My answer was, "I have no words. Sawaki Roshi isn't dangerous anymore. But we are still dangerous."

I'm a Japanese Buddhist and Sawaki Roshi's Dharma descendant. I think whatever I say in defense, apology, or criticism could be biased. I don't think Sawaki Roshi was a warmonger, but it's true that he didn't oppose the imperial system, and so to a certain degree we have to accept the fact that he supported the war. He was conditioned as a Japanese man born in that time. I respect him and value his way of life—free of fame and profit—and his devotion to zazen practice. But I also think to worship Sawaki Roshi or any teacher without critical thinking is dangerous. Sawaki Roshi and other Japanese Buddhist leaders, orders, and teachings must be critically studied and objectively evaluated—as should all teachers, from all times and places.

When I asked Uchiyama Roshi to take me as his disciple, he advised me to consider him an "anti-role model." I assumed he meant because he sat with the monks only during sesshin and Sunday gatherings; he couldn't sit with us every day because of his health.

I think we need this same attitude when we study Sawaki Roshi's or any Zen master's life.

Acknowledgments

Rev. Jisho Warner and Rev. Shoryu Bradley took time out of their busy lives to look at this manuscript in the final stage and gave us many helpful suggestions. I appreciate their kindness and love for the Dharma.

I would like to offer special thanks to Michael Hofmann for his longtime friendship. He painted the portaits of Sawaki Roshi, Uchiyama Roshi, and me for this book. His wonderful paintings express my teachers' strong but gentle, strict but flexible, and warm personalities. In the early 1970s, he met Zenkei Shibayama Roshi and went to Japan to practice Zen and study *sumie* painting with well-known painter Gyokusei Jikihara, chairman of the Japan Nanga Academy. Because Shibayama Roshi knew Uchiyama Roshi, Michael began to come to Antaiji to sit. That was around the time I started to study English. He was my first English tutor. He visited Antaiji once a week to talk with me in English. When I first came to the U.S. in 1975, Michael and his girlfriend, Arthur Braverman and his wife, and my Dharma brother Rev. Eishin Ikeda and I traveled from California to Massachusetts through the South in Michael's VW bus, on which he had painted Bodhidharma and the Second Ancestor, Huike. That was one of the most impressive travel experiences of my life. Thanks to the friendship of many Americans practicing at Antaiji, including Michael, I could continue to practice in this country to today.

Finally, I'd like to express my deep gratitude to Daihorinkaku, the Japanese Buddhist publisher, for their kind permission to translate this book.

Introduction
by Kosho Uchiyama

In the fall of 1965, Mr. Toshio Yamada, then editor of the religious column in the *Asahi Shimbun*, visited Antaiji to inquire about Sawaki Roshi's health. On that occasion he said, "Sawaki Roshi always talks straightforwardly, and many people are deeply impressed. Could you write some articles about how you as his disciple understand his teachings?" I thought writing these articles would be good for me as part of my practice.

I reviewed Sawaki Roshi's sharp and profound sayings from his lectures, which I had recorded in my notebooks as "Dharma words" (or *hokku*) of Homeless (or *Yadonashi*) Kodo. Then I began to write my comments on them, like a conversation with my teacher. I entitled this commentary *Yadonashi Hokku-san*, or *Appreciating the Dharma Words of Homeless Kodo*.

However, that fall Sawaki Roshi suddenly became critically ill, and I couldn't continue the project. He passed away at the end of the year. Unexpectedly my articles became a memorial address and were published serially in the religious column of the Osaka *Asahi* newspaper every Sunday, starting from the second week of January 1966. This continued for one year and two months; I wrote fifty-six articles. Writing them not only gave me a chance to deepen my appreciation of Sawaki Roshi's teachings but also comforted and encouraged me when I was lonely because of the death of my teacher, whom I relied on. I was extremely grateful to Mr. Yamada for giving me this opportunity.

The fifty-six articles were compiled into two booklets published by Hakujusha Press. For the seventh anniversary of Sawaki Roshi's death, Mr. Nakayama, president of Hakujusha, asked me to write some additional articles to create a book. I thought it would be nice to publish this book as a memorial to Sawaki Roshi. So I wrote fifteen more articles.

As many people knew, Sawaki Roshi was like a typical ancient Zen master: dynamic, fearless, and unconventional. It's rare to see teachers like him these days. I, on the contrary, am such a fainthearted person that I hesitate to tell people I was his disciple. Yet I practiced with him longer than anyone and served as his closest disciple. Near the end of his life, I asked him, "I am such a weak person. Is it possible for me to lead people after your death?" He replied, "In our tradition, zazen is the most honored one. As long as you continue to practice zazen, you can lead people without mistake." He encouraged his cowardly disciple and showed me the path to take.

I received this as his final teaching. Since then, I have devoted myself to zazen and have maintained Antaiji as a place where the practice of zazen is the most honored.

This book is a collection of the responses of his timid disciple to the Dharma expressions of Sawaki Roshi's dynamic personality. Precisely because of this, the book might be helpful in introducing Sawaki Roshi's teaching to readers and allowing them to feel more comfortable with it. Indeed, there are more fearful people like me in this world than courageous ones like him.

It is with deep gratitude that I offer this book.

Remembering his final days
On this day in early autumn,
Close to the seventh anniversary of his death.

The Zen Teaching of Homeless Kodo

1.

No Need to Be Chained

KODO SAWAKI:
People call me Homeless Kodo, but I don't think they particularly intend to disparage me. They say "homeless" probably because I never had a temple or owned a house. Anyway, all human beings without exception are in reality homeless. It's a mistake to think we have a solid home.

KOSHO UCHIYAMA:
I've selected some of Sawaki Roshi's Dharma words from my notebooks, which I kept while I practiced with him for twenty-five years. I'd like to savor them together with readers.

It wasn't necessarily comfortable for me, as his disciple, that Sawaki Roshi was called Homeless Kodo. The word *homeless* has associations with stray dogs and alley cats. However, if all human beings are actually homeless, this nickname can be understood as an honorific title for a person who lives in accordance with reality.

As a disciple of a "homeless" teacher, I myself was homeless. I had to get daily food and provisions through *takuhatsu*, religious begging. Dogs often threatened me. Once a spitz jumped up and barked viciously. The chain tied to the dog's collar wasn't tight enough, and suddenly it came undone. The dog immediately cowered, whined, and retreated. It seems a dog barks overbearingly when chained, but loses nerve as soon as it's free.

It was entertaining to see that the dog behaved like some human beings. However, it's rather pitiful when humans act like that dog. Some people high-handedly bark at others while they're leashed by financial power, social status, or organizational authority, but as soon as the chains are removed they become gutless and powerless, and they retreat. Such people are truly miserable. I hope to be a person who can live majestically while "homeless."

For human beings, it's best to be without chains.

SHOHAKU OKUMURA:
This is the first article Uchiyama Roshi wrote in his series of weekly newspaper columns titled *Yadonashi Hokku-san*. *Hokku* literally means "Dharma phrases." This word is used as the translation of the title of one of the oldest and most well-known Buddhist scriptures in the Pali canon: the Dhammapada. As he writes in chapter 8 of this book, Uchiyama Roshi intended this series of columns to be the Dhammapada of modern times.

Yadonashi, or "homeless," was Sawaki Roshi's nickname, and in the Zen tradition, *san* means to meet a teacher to study and practice. So the title means studying and digesting the Dharma words of the homeless Zen master.

Sawaki Roshi's nickname was coined by Rev. Yuho Hosokawa of the Buddhist publishing house Daihorinkaku, who edited the collection of Sawaki Roshi's talks. When the editor had to contact Roshi, it was often difficult to find him because he was always traveling to teach. Sawaki Roshi called his style of teaching a "moving monastery." When his editor called one place, they said, "Roshi was here but left several days ago." Or "We expect Roshi soon, but he's not here yet." At that time, not many people in Japan had telephones. If Sawaki Roshi had known cell phones, I'm sure he would have considered them a leash.

Yadonashi refers to people removed from the census during the Tokugawa period. Some were criminals, while many others were farmers who left their home villages because of natural disasters or other reasons. They were considered outcasts. The label *yadonashi* had very negative connotations. However, if we interpret this expression in the context of Mahayana Buddhism, it refers to one of the three kinds of nirvana: *mujusho nehan*, the nirvana of no abiding. Bodhisattvas do not abide in samsara because of wisdom and do not rest in nirvana because of compassion.

2.

Having Finally Returned to a
True Way of Life

KODO SAWAKI:

A religion that has nothing to do with our fundamental attitude toward our lives is nonsense. Buddhadharma is a religion that teaches us how to return to a true way of life. "Subduing non-Buddhists," or converting people, means helping them transform their lives from a half-baked, incomplete way to a genuine way.

KOSHO UCHIYAMA:

More than fourteen hundred years have passed since Buddhism was first transmitted to Japan. There's something surprising in the achievements of Buddhist monks during this long history: they've never taught Japanese people the essence of Buddhism as a religion. In no other field of endeavor can a person waste time like this; if a pilot fails to operate an airplane, the plane will crash. But if a priest makes a mistake chanting sutras during a funeral, the deceased will not complain. Probably this is why priests can get away with laziness.

Sawaki Roshi comes directly to the heart of the matter and says in a living, modern language, "Buddhadharma is a religion that allows us to live a genuine life." From the time of Shakyamuni, Buddhism should have simply taught this point. Nevertheless, in the history of Buddhism, too much emphasis has been put on various ridiculous superstitions, and this fundamental point has been lost. We should reflect whether we are living our lives with an unshakably stable attitude. Please savor the following Dharma words.

KODO SAWAKI:

Most people don't act based on penetrating insights into their lives. They do things in a makeshift way, like putting a bandaid on their shoulder when they have soreness.

To be born human is rare, and we should be grateful and use our lives meaningfully. It's absurd to get depressed because you don't have money. It's rubbish to become neurotic simply because you're not sitting in a VIP seat. It's foolish to cry merely because you were rejected by your girlfriend. Rather, having been born human, we should live a life worth living.

SHOHAKU OKUMURA:

"Religion" is a translation of the Japanese word *shukyo*. *Shukyo* literally means teaching (*kyo*) about the ultimate truth (*shu*)—the truth to which the Buddha awakened, and his teachings on this truth. Because Sawaki Roshi and Uchiyama Roshi use *shukyo* with this original meaning, the English word *religion* might cause confusion.

Of course, Uchiyama Roshi exaggerates somewhat in saying Japanese Buddhist monks have failed to teach the essence of Buddhism. There have been great Buddhist masters, such as Dogen Zenji and others, and many sincere monks and lay Buddhists. However it's true that Buddhist monks have mainly taught worship of buddhas and bodhisattvas for worldly benefit; doing good and avoiding evil to be reborn in heaven rather than hell; and ancestor worship through funerals, memorial services, and other ceremonies.

Is it fair to call all these activities superstitions? Some priests in traditional Buddhist institutions, as well as some scholars of religion and cultural anthropology, wouldn't agree with Uchiyama Roshi. But Sawaki Roshi and Uchiyama Roshi are speaking from the "homeless" practitioner's perspective, which has nothing to do with religious institutions or ordinary religious culture. For them, *shukyo* simply means to study, practice, and live the fundamental truth. Even when they're respected, such people have often been considered outsiders within religious institutions. For example, Rev. Reirin Yamada, a former president of Komazawa University who later became abbot of Eiheiji monastery said, "Sawaki Roshi was a respectable Zen master. But because he spoke ill of Buddhist priests, I didn't like him."

"Having finally returned to a true way of life" is a translation of Sawaki Roshi's expression *ikituku tokoro e ikituita jinsei,* or "the way of life having reached where we should reach." Since this is unique wording, it's difficult to translate. Uchiyama Roshi fully discusses this expression in an essay toward the end of this book, "Kodo Sawaki Roshi's Zazen." When he first listened to Sawaki Roshi's lectures, Uchiyama Roshi thought this was the essential point of Sawaki Roshi's teaching. The expression conveys Sawaki Roshi's understanding of Dogen Zenji's teaching that "we take refuge in Buddha, Dharma, and Sangha because these three are the place we finally return." I think this expression also has the connotation of *paramita,* perfection, or crossing the boundary between samsara and nirvana. We practice not to get somewhere better. We practice here and now, transcending the distinction between samsara and nirvana.

This expression is also associated with the Lotus Sutra parable of a rich father and his poor son. The son left home when young and wandered here and there seeking clothing and food, sometimes receiving, sometimes not. Sawaki Roshi considers our makeshift way of life in samsara like the destitute son's wandering. To practice zazen is to return to our true home and settle there.

It's important to consider this chapter and the previous one together. Sawaki Roshi's way of life was without a fixed home, yet his attitude toward life was resolute. He said, "I don't grow rice, I don't compose poems; I know what I do."

3.

What Is Efficiency For?

KODO SAWAKI:
Some students cheat in preparatory schools so they can get into college. But such students will also need to cheat to pass their university entrance exams. The degree of their stupidity is twisted and perverse; it's ridiculously blind. However, our entire world today is engaged in the same kind of stupidity.

KOSHO UCHIYAMA:
All human beings are very short-sighted at certain points. Because a luxury car is a symbol of wealth, some people borrow large amounts of money to buy such cars. To help his corrupt boss rise, a faithful lackey will take blame for him even if it means going to jail. We tend to do things without understanding why we're doing them or which direction we want to go. Not only a few individuals: the whole world in this age puts primary emphasis on increasing efficiency in every area of life. But where are we going, and what's the goal of all these attempts? No matter how much we speed up everything and work more efficiently, unless we choose the right direction, what's the difference between human beings and maggots that automatically start wriggling in spring? The Chinese character for "working" (働) is different from "moving" (動). The left side of the character for "human" (人) must be added to transform random movements into work.

It's true that science and technology have greatly developed. But this is nothing more than just that: the development of science and technology. We need to make a clear distinction between material development and human progress. We should rethink what is true progress for human beings in its deepest meaning.

KODO SAWAKI:

Because of developments in transportation, we feel planet Earth is getting smaller and smaller. But where are we going in our speedy cars? We play pinball; we gamble. We move so fast simply to do wasteful things.

"I sat up all night playing mah-jong." Some people take vitamins so they can overdo, almost tearfully, with red eyes.

SHOHAKU OKUMURA:

Sawaki Roshi's comment about cheating in preparatory schools is probably a joke. As a professor at Komazawa University for almost thirty years, he knew the students and the system very well. In Japan the educational system was and still is very competitive. It's difficult to enter prestigious universities; this was especially true while the baby boomers were coming of age in the 1960s and '70s. Many students who failed to enter universities had to attend preparatory schools to train to retake the entrance exams the next year. They studied merely to pass these exams and often took practice tests. Sawaki Roshi says that some students cheated on these mock exams, even though good scores on these tests meant nothing for their success on the real exams. They were driven to cheat by their competitive minds, thinking only of the test in front of them and not seeing that the score didn't even matter. This is an example of extremely nearsighted activity.

In the 1960s, some people began to realize that materialism based on mass production and consumption might be as much of a threat to human existence as the Cold War and nuclear weapons. But half a century after Sawaki Roshi and Uchiyama Roshi warned that we need to change the direction of civilization and understand what progress means for human beings, we're still puzzled. Many people now agree we need to make changes, but it seems we don't know how yet.

After Japan's earthquake of March 2011, people have been rethinking the relationship between human beings and nature, and the way we live. We recognize how small and weak we are compared to the power of nature. And yet, we tend to think we own this planet and we can do anything we want to make our lives more prosperous, comfortable, and enjoyable. One of the Buddha's important teachings is to scale down our desires and know how much is enough. I discuss this further in chapter 33.

Seeing with Fresh Eyes

KODO SAWAKI:

When you steal other people's belongings, you become a thief. This is very simple and clear. But people today think one becomes a criminal only after being arrested by a policeman, investigated by a prosecutor, sentenced by a judge, and confined in a prison. Therefore, corrupt politicians think they are men of virtue and skill if they can cover up their deeds and escape getting caught. They are heavily influenced by "group stupidity."

Alexander the Great, Julius Caesar, and Genghis Khan were nothing other than great thieves. Hitler and Mussolini were greater robbers than the legendary thieves Ishikawa Goemon and Tenichibo. Although these dictators operated on a much larger scale, they were not fundamentally different from Kunisada Chuji, who said, "Let's go as far as we can, no matter what." And yet the henchmen of thieves think their bosses are respected.

We're always falling into ruts. Politicians and their followers, many schoolteachers, and opinion leaders work hard to manipulate people into biased, habitual ways of thinking. The ways we're distorted are subtle, deliberate, and complicated. When we're liberated from this distortion, we will find the true wisdom of Buddhism.

KOSHO UCHIYAMA:

Japanese today are forced to be stupid. Sawaki Roshi called it "group stupidity." It would be fine if prime ministers and other political, economic, and cultural leaders were truly esteemed people. But it's a problem if they're powerful only within the framework of conventional distortion. Buddhadharma is a religion that allows practitioners to open clear and fresh eyes, unimpaired by habitual ways of thinking. To clarify the warped and deadly situation in Japanese politics, each and every one of us must open our eyes and criticize current conditions. Buddhism in its true meaning must be a living teaching in these times.

SHOHAKU OKUMURA:
"Group stupidity" is one of the important expressions coined by Sawaki Roshi. Uchiyama Roshi discusses this symptom of mass society in chapters 11 through 17. Because of the development of mass media—television, newspapers, magazines, and the internet—we're manipulated and controlled by other people's opinions without even knowing it. Although this is better than a dictatorship in which no one can express their opinions, it has its own dangers.

Ishikawa Goemon (1558–94) was a famous thief during the Azuchi-Momoyama period. Tenichibo (1699–1729) lied that he was a son of the shogun and recruited unemployed samurai, saying that he would become a lord. He was executed by the government. Kunisada Chuji (1810–50) was a gambler. He killed many people to gain power in the world of outlaws. In Japanese stories and movies, these criminals are sometimes considered heroes, but Sawaki Roshi considered them examples of ego-centered ways of life. They stole, deceived, and fought for their own profit. Sawaki Roshi compared these small-time crooks with world leaders, because while many people worship dictators as heroes, such figures merely occupy positions of power. We can consider Shakyamuni and other Buddhist masters as examples of an opposite kind of hero, who renounced wealth, power, and privilege for the sake of the Dharma.

5.

The Greatness of Sawaki Roshi

KODO SAWAKI:
Someone once said, "Sawaki Roshi wasted his entire life on zazen."

KOSHO UCHIYAMA:
This was Sawaki Roshi's self-appraisal in a series titled *The Unpainted Face*, published in the *Asahi* newspaper.

Sawaki Roshi passed away on December 21, 1965. Afterward many of his followers visited Antaiji to burn incense in his honor. All of them praised his greatness, but most didn't remember him as a person who wasted his entire life on zazen.

One said, "Sawaki Roshi defeated General Ugaki with a single word." Another reminisced, "When he encountered old Mr. Matsunaga, Roshi did such and such." Still another commented, "When I asked him about the Suez Canal affair, I was very impressed with his answer, although I didn't quite understand what he meant. He said, 'You should cover the canal with Buddha's robe.'"

In too many stories I didn't even understand why these people admired Sawaki Roshi. It's true that he was a courageous soldier during the Russo-Japanese War and was awarded the Golden Kite for his distinguished service. He always said, "As a daredevil, I was second to none." However, at the same time, he added, "This is only the greatness of Mori no Ishimatsu," the famously reckless gambler.

From his birth, Sawaki Roshi was a vital and charismatic person who dominated others and yet attracted them like a magnet. Yet this was merely a karmic attribute, as natural for him as a cat catching mice or a musk deer emitting an appealing fragrance. This cannot be his greatness as Buddhadharma. Sooner or later a collection of anecdotes about his life will be published; I'd like to make sure they merely entertain people as interesting stories, without confusing them about the meaning of Buddhadharma.

Sometimes we fail to praise a person for his or her true virtue. In this case, Sawaki Roshi's karmic attributes have nothing to do with his way of life as a person who "wasted his entire life on zazen."

SHOHAKU OKUMURA:

If he hadn't become a Buddhist monk, Sawaki Roshi would have been successful in a worldly sense in business, politics, or the military. Instead, he devoted his life to wholeheartedly practicing Dogen Zenji's just sitting, or *shikantaza*, which according to him was good for nothing. For him, social climbing in pursuit of fame and profit was meaningless.

The Japanese expression for "waste" is *bonifuru*, which means "sacrifice," "lose all," or "ruin." So when we say he wasted his life, we use the expression in a paradoxical way—like saying that zazen is good for nothing. These sayings point to a standard beyond worldly values.

General Ugaki refers to Kazushige Ugaki (1868–1956), minister of the army in the 1930s. Old Mr. Matsunaga refers to Yasuzaemon Matsunaga (1875–1971), a famous businessman who managed several electric companies. Sawaki Roshi was well-known for anecdotes involving noted politicians, military people, and businessmen. He often prevailed over those with power, fame, and authority and yet was admired by them. Here Uchiyama Roshi emphasizes that this celebrated aspect of Sawaki Roshi's personality had nothing to do with his life as a practitioner of Buddhadharma. Sawaki Roshi followed Dogen Zenji's admonition to practice only for the sake of Dharma, without any gaining mind.

6

Returning to the Self

KODO SAWAKI:
We cannot exchange even a fart with another, can we? Each and every one of us has to live out our self. Who's better looking, who's smarter: you or I? We don't need to compare ourselves with others.

KOSHO UCHIYAMA:
Sawaki Roshi spent his entire life devoted to zazen. What is this zazen that he expounded? In his early days, he often said, "Zazen is the self selfing the self" or "To practice zazen is to be intimate with the self." In short, in our daily lives, we always worry about our relations with others, and we're absorbed in competition with them. To practice zazen is to let go of these comparisons and just sit, being the self that is only the self.

Soon, the season for final exams and entrance exams will come. Some students will commit suicide because of bad grades or failure on these exams. This is a tragedy caused by our educational system, in which students are taught merely to compete with others. They are never taught to return to the self, which is the most important thing.

Whether we defeat others or are defeated, we live out the self that is only the self. There's no way to become someone else. So we should return to the self with peace of mind. This is the practice of zazen, in which we sit "letting go of all associations, and putting all affairs aside," as Dogen's *Fukanzazengi* says.

In the Sutta Nipata, Shakyamuni Buddha said, "Make yourself your refuge, walk in the world, and be unchained from everything." In Genjokoan, Dogen Zenji wrote, "To study the buddha way is to study the self." Without being pulled every which way by comparing yourself with others, settle down within your self in its true meaning. This is the essential way that Buddhadharma pacifies our minds. And this is the most genuine zazen practice.

KODO SAWAKI:
Sit immovably in the place where being superior or inferior to others doesn't matter.

SHOHAKU OKUMURA:
When Uchiyama Roshi wrote this article in 1966, I was a high school student, and I was attracted by his comments on Japanese education. I wasn't happy at school. Education was very competitive. I was taught by my parents and teachers to study hard to enter a prestigious university. When I asked why, their answer was this: so I could get a good job, achieve a higher status on society's ladder, and make a lot of money. To me, all of Japanese society seemed like a huge money-making machine, with school as the factory producing the parts of this machine. If I became a good and useful part, my life would be happy and successful. Otherwise, my life would be a failure. I couldn't find any meaning in that life. I wanted an alternative way of living. Sawaki Roshi and Uchiyama Roshi seemed to understand my reservations about the educational system. I'm deeply grateful that I encountered their way of life and became their student.

Nearly fifty years later, Japan has become one of the richest countries in the world, but more than thirty thousand Japanese commit suicide each year. I'm convinced the system that demands young people work hard, compete, and get rich hasn't made the Japanese happy in the long run.

Excessive competition is unwholesome for winners as well as losers. Those who lose may suffer a sense of inferiority, but winners also experience unhealthy effects, such as arrogance that hinders them from working harmoniously with others. And when they finally encounter people superior to them, they can't escape their sense of inferiority. I hope school can become a place where young people can nurture their life force in a healthy way, enabling them to live on equal ground with each other.

7.

Circumstances

KODO SAWAKI:
These days, young hoodlums often say they committed crimes because of their abusive childhoods and awful circumstances. Which kind of upbringing is good, and which is bad, after all? Is being born poor good? Is being born rich bad? The problem is that even though you were born human, you haven't found your true self, the way you really wish to live. That's a terrible circumstance!

KOSHO UCHIYAMA:
In his final year, Sawaki Roshi often talked about his stepfather. I was always deeply moved when I listened to these stories. When Sawaki Roshi was five, his mother died, and his father died a few years later. After that, he was adopted by Bunkichi Sawaki. Bunkichi was ostensibly a paper lantern maker, but actually he was a professional gambler. As soon as Sawaki Roshi was adopted, he was forced to serve as lookout for the police. Young as he was, Roshi was astounded by this. His circumstances were the back streets of the red-light district.

When he returned home from the Russo-Japanese War because of a nearly fatal wound, Sawaki Roshi found that his adoptive mother, a former prostitute, had lost her mind. She was chained and smeared with her own shit. His adoptive father had gone out gambling. When he came back he said, "My wife has gone crazy, and I'm broke. I don't know what to do. Give me some money!"

Despite such early circumstances, Sawaki Roshi lived his life devoted to the Buddhadharma. The comment above expresses his irritation with the excuses of young people. At the same time, this perspective has limitless relevance for many of us who feel bound by the circumstances of our personal lives.

SHOHAKU OKUMURA:
This is a concrete example of liberation from karma, of how it's possible to transform our lives from the conditioning of our upbringing and situation.

Sawaki Roshi was from poor and cruel circumstances and became a devoted practitioner for his entire life. In contrast, Shakyamuni Buddha was a crown prince raised in luxury. It's said that his father, King Suddhodana, feared his son might leave home to become a monk, so he provided everything his child might want. Nevertheless, the young prince renounced his life of ease to devote himself to the Buddhadharma. Dogen Zenji was also from a prestigious, aristocratic family. For such people, leaving home and becoming spiritual practitioners living in intentional poverty must have been very difficult.

Like Dogen Zenji, Uchiyama Roshi was born into a relatively wealthy family. His father owned a company until he went bankrupt. Uchiyama Roshi said he never washed even a handkerchief by himself until he became a monk. He was a very intellectual, physically weak person. He was almost the opposite of Sawaki Roshi, who had little formal education but was physically very strong. Since these spiritual practitioners came from very different karmic backgrounds, we shouldn't complain about our own circumstances or feel trapped by them.

When I moved from Japan to western Massachusetts at twenty-seven, I spoke English poorly and was a city boy who didn't know anything about living in the woods. I felt like a five-year-old. I had to learn everything again. I couldn't live and practice the way I was trained in Japan. It was very difficult, but by surviving these challenges, I was liberated to a certain degree from my karmic tendencies and my conditioned self-image.

8

Creating Sutras

KODO SAWAKI:

A home-leaver should be a person who creates a unique way of life.

KOSHO UCHIYAMA:

Sawaki Roshi was always saying this. His "homeless" life was his original creation. And expounding Dharma in a profound and resonant way using simple colloquial expressions instead of Buddhist technical terms was his distinctive teaching style.

However, if I as his disciple merely imitate his way of life or repeat his sayings, I will be acting contrary to my teacher's spirit. To be a faithful Dharma heir, I need to go beyond Roshi's way of life to create my own life and expressions of the Dharma.

Another thing Sawaki Roshi often said was, "All the Buddhist sutras are only footnotes to zazen." After Roshi's death, I wished to continue practicing zazen with his spirit. I vowed to develop sutras for modern people using contemporary language to convey how zazen can offer guidance in our complicated time.

Today, Buddhism in Japan has stagnated. I think this is because priests and scholars merely interpret the old scriptures. No one writes sutras for modern times. At the beginning of the Common Era, for several centuries zazen practitioners produced enormous numbers of Mahayana sutras that were lively and filled with genuine spirit. Thanks to them, Mahayana Buddhism blossomed. Today, I want to declare a new age for the creation of Buddhist sutras. I'm writing this series of essays on Sawaki Roshi's Dharma phrases with this aspiration.

Religion loses its vitality when people simply follow fixed doctrines and maintain religious institutions. Only when we seek the truth of our selves and create our own spiritual life can we give birth to the potential that can point the way for our time.

SHOHAKU OKUMURA:

Sutras originally refers to a category of Buddhist scriptures considered to be the record of Shakyamuni Buddha's teachings. Mahayana sutras began to be produced around the first century BCE, a few hundred years after Buddha's death. Commonly the word *sutras* is also used to refer to all Buddhist scriptures, including commentaries and texts about precepts. Here Uchiyama Roshi uses the word in this broad meaning.

Until the end of the nineteenth century, Japanese Buddhists only studied scriptures that had been transmitted from China. These days in the U.S. we can study texts in English translation from almost all Buddhist traditions, including Chinese, Tibetan, and Theravada—the Pali Canon, for instance. Teachings based on these texts are compared with other spiritual traditions such as Christianity, Judaism, Islam, and Hinduism. Traditional Buddhist teachings are interpreted and practiced in the context of modern physics, psychology, environmentalism, social activism, and other fields. These activities can be considered the evolution of Buddhist sutras for modern times.

What I can offer to this new stage of Buddhism is introducing Dogen Zenji and his tradition, Soto Zen—including Sawaki Roshi's and Uchiyama Roshi's teachings—to the West. My wish is to make this wisdom understandable to people of the twenty-first century.

9

What Is Happiness?

KODO SAWAKI:

A horse and a cat once discussed the question, "What is happiness?" They couldn't reach any agreement.

KOSHO UCHIYAMA:

There's a new religion that's enthusiastic about gaining converts. When they approach people, they abruptly ask, "Are you happy?" This question surely touches a vulnerability in human beings. We're always pursuing happiness. And yet we cannot always be in a trance of happiness, like sweethearts newly fallen in love—that's not a normal condition.

Usually people hesitate in answering this simple and direct question. So the recruiters say, "Join our religion, and you'll be happy." Then they fire question after question and offer seductive arguments to persuade people to join their cult.

In such a situation, we'd like to have the wits to turn the question back to the other person: "What's happiness for you?" We should be clear which definition of happiness they're talking about. If they say, "Happiness is being wealthy, important, and healthy," then when we die, all of us will be in the pit of misery. Death is a time when our money, status, and health are taken away.

As long as we view happiness within the duality of fortune-misfortune and in terms of our ever-changing emotions, we'll be divided within ourselves like the horse and cat, and will never reach a conclusion.

KODO SAWAKI:

Peace and joy in the mundane world change into suffering and pain sooner or later. Today's fortune becomes tomorrow's misfortune.

To be good-looking is not necessarily to be happy. There was a beautiful woman who attracted many men and therefore gave birth to three fatherless kids, whom she had to struggle to support.

Even when people love each other, there's no guarantee their love will continue for their entire lives. There was a couple who loved each other and yet, since it wasn't possible to marry, tried to commit suicide. But one of them survived and fell in love with someone else. Humans are really troublesome.

SHOHAKU OKUMURA:

Usually happiness is defined as a condition in which all of one's desires are satisfied. Most of us have desires for wealth, social status, fame, health, etc. In Buddha's teaching, those in the most fortunate conditions are called heavenly beings. Yet in Buddhism the various heavens are still part of the six realms of samsara—that is, the realms of suffering. When the Buddha said everything is suffering, conditions in these heavens were included.

This means the duality of sadness and happiness is the basic cause of suffering. Cessation of suffering, which is nirvana, means going beyond this duality of misery and joy. The Buddha taught the path to freedom from desires, not the way to satisfy them. Mahayana Buddhism teaches that bodhisattvas should transcend even the dichotomy of samsara and nirvana.

Right now, right here, in whatever condition, whether hell or heaven, just keep practicing steadily, led by the bodhisattva vows:

> Beings are numberless; I vow to free them.
> Delusions are inexhaustible; I vow to end them.
> Dharma gates are boundless; I vow to enter them.
> The buddha way is unsurpassable; I vow to realize it.

This is what Sawaki Roshi means by living a true and stable life.

10

Making Human Beings into Commodities

KODO SAWAKI:

Today's educational system is wrong and causes trouble. Schools examine and grade students, classifying human beings and assigning them numbers. There's nothing more ridiculous. Who on earth is superior? Who's inferior? Is it superior to have a good memory and inferior to have a poor one? Aren't there many foolish people with good memories?

Moreover, if a person is given low grades, they might be caught in an inferiority complex for their entire life and think, "I'm no good." But actually it's this system of classification, and our internalization of it, that is no good.

KOSHO UCHIYAMA:

The most popular hostess at a nightclub might think proudly, "I'm number one." However, she sometimes feels loneliness and emptiness within this favorable condition because she finds that she's simply the most expensive commodity for sale in the store's showcase. No matter how expensively she's sold, the moment she discovers deep in her mind that she's just a commodity, she'll naturally feel empty.

Are schools merely factories to produce commodities called human beings? It seems the only purpose of an education is to make its products more valuable commercially. Elementary school is simply preparation for the exam to enter a good middle school. Middle school is merely to pass the exam for a better high school. High school is just preparation for a prestigious university. Attending university is simply to get a desirable job at a big company. Students are placed on a conveyor belt as goods to be sold. I suppose some student violence is resistance against a society in which human beings are treated like commodities. Violence and feelings of inferiority are two symptoms of our competitive society.

KODO SAWAKI:
Studying originally meant aspiring to discover the meaning of life. These days studying has become all about getting a job.

SHOHAKU OKUMURA:
This is another example of what attracted me as a high school student to Sawaki Roshi and Uchiyama Roshi. When I became interested in Zen and Buddhism, the most famous writer about Zen was D. T. Suzuki (1870–1966). I tried to read one of his books but gave up after a few pages. To a high school student, he was as difficult as Dogen. However, Sawaki Roshi's and Uchiyama Roshi's teachings spoke directly to the problems I was facing as a teenager in the 1960s.

Uchiyama Roshi wrote three books about education. One is titled *Jinseika-dokuhon*, or *Textbook on Studying Human Life*. He wished to teach the truth of human life to high school students. He contended that in the modern age, competition for survival is the basic principle of society, and education is based on this principle. But he insisted that students should be taught how to live based on their life force. People should exist not as interchangeable parts of an economic machine but as human beings who live and die, impermanent and irreplaceable, each with our own beauty. He often said a real flower is beautiful because of its impermanence, which a plastic flower lacks.

Another of his books was a collection of essays for teachers. He encouraged them to teach students that we live together not only with other people but also with all living beings, and we should respect and value the life we share.

Group Stupidity's Relevance Today

KODO SAWAKI:

When people are alone, they're not so bad. However, when a group forms, paralysis occurs; people become totally foolish and cannot distinguish good from bad. Their minds are numbed by the group. Because of their desire to belong and even to lose themselves, some pay membership fees. Others work on advertising to attract people and intoxicate them for some political, spiritual, or commercial purpose.

I keep some distance from society, not to escape it but to avoid this kind of paralysis. To practice zazen is to become free of this group stupidity.

KOSHO UCHIYAMA:

In Buddhism, the obstacle that causes suffering in our lives is called "delusive desire": in Sanskrit, *klesha*, and in Japanese, *bonno*. Which desire is considered the worst hindrance has differed depending on time and place. In ancient India, people thought the most troublesome obstacle for practitioners was sexual desire. They made strong efforts to control such desires. Later, in *Shobogenzo Gyoji*, Dogen Zenji said, "The desire for fame is worse than violating the precepts." He considered pursuing fame and profit the greatest hindrance to practice, probably because in his time, monks in Nara and on Mount Koya and Mount Hiei competed with each other for wealth and renown.

Sexual greed and desire for fame and profit are all obstacles that should be renounced by practitioners of the buddha way. When Sawaki Roshi coined the expression "group stupidity," he was speaking of hindrances not only for Buddhist practitioners but for everyone in this modern age.

Because of this, Buddhist teaching resonates beyond the circle of the Buddhist community and gains relevance for our contemporary society. Today people live relying on groups and organizations, drifting along in them like floating weeds without roots. Buddhism can help people awaken from the haze of group stupidity and open the clear eyes of the self.

SHOHAKU OKUMURA:

Sawaki Roshi coined many unique expressions. Among them, Uchiyama Roshi values "group stupidity" as a phrase that identifies the fundamental obstacle to people in our modern society. This is a difficult expression to translate into English. The original Japanese is *grupuboke*. *Bokeru* means our minds stop functioning in a normal, wholesome way because of internal or external conditions such as intoxication, disorder, illness, aging, etc. Sawaki Roshi observes that when people identify with a group or organization, their minds stop working in a healthy way.

I'm not sure whether Sawaki Roshi invented the expression "group stupidity" specifically for modern people. This is not only a modern phenomenon. A group-oriented mentality has existed in Japanese culture since ancient times. I think it was Uchiyama Roshi's insight that interpreted Sawaki Roshi's admonitions on "group stupidity" as a warning for modern times.

In my high school library, I found *The Organization Man* by William H. Whyte. I didn't understand it very well at the time, but the title and at least one point I gathered impressed me; I remember thinking I didn't want to be an organization man. Recently, I recalled the book. I researched it online and found a description that said, "An organization man is an employee, especially of a large corporation, who has adapted so completely to what is expected in attitudes, ideas, behavior, etc. by the corporation as to have lost a sense of personal identity or independence."

It seems Uchiyama Roshi had the same insight as William Whyte about how people working for organizations lose their identity. And this is the majority of modern people—in the twenty-first century, it seems the entire human world is becoming one huge corporation.

12

Mob Psychology

KODO SAWAKI:

Mob psychology is funny. If people don't understand a situation, they should keep quiet. But instead they say and do things, heedlessly following what they don't know, without convictions of their own. They don't see with the clear eyes of the self at all. This is called *ukiyo*, the floating world.

Even if you do something brave, if you do it merely because of being caught up in excitement, it cannot be called a truly brave deed.

Don't lose your head in crazy circumstances. Don't be intoxicated by atmosphere. This is true wisdom. Do not be won over to any idea, or "ism," or any organization. Do not engage in the human foolishness of discrimination.

KOSHO UCHIYAMA:

A member of the imperial family once said that Japanese get stressed easily. It seems true that we often become anxious about nothing particularly important and act with our nerves on edge. Moreover, when we're in a crowd, each person's tension influences others, who become more and more keyed up, and we lose ourselves. Intoxicated by the group atmosphere, we may do the most unexpected things, which would never happen if we were alone and sober.

Student uproar is a good example. I can understand how easily students are swept away; I myself was a student during the strike at Waseda University in 1931, and I watched the movement from within. In such a situation, regardless of which side is right or wrong, or how things are going, I recommend that instead of making inflammatory appeals, the parties hang a banner on the clock tower reading, "IF YOU DO SOMETHING BRAVE MERELY BECAUSE OF BEING CAUGHT UP IN EXCITEMENT, IT CANNOT BE CALLED A TRULY BRAVE DEED," or "DON'T LOSE YOUR HEAD IN CRAZY CIRCUMSTANCES," or "DON'T BE INTOXICATED BY THE ATMOSPHERE." It would be better to argue and negotiate with such banners in view.

KODO SAWAKI:

Our practice of zazen is looking at the world afresh after being in hibernation.

It's best to do zazen without doing anything else. When we do something else, too often we're made to do it by a demon.

SHOHAKU OKUMURA:

Uchiyama Roshi wrote his words in 1966 during another struggle at Waseda. This was the forerunner of the strife at many universities that continued until the early seventies. At first, students were protesting how schools were managed, but these protests turned political, against the government and business leaders supporting "American Imperialism," particularly the Vietnam War. These student movements were organized by left-wing political parties such as the Socialists or Communists, and some students didn't like being connected with these parties. Within the student population there were many factions, and they started to fight.

I went to Tokyo in 1968 to attend Komazawa University and study Buddhism. The same thing happened there in my first and second years. First, students occupied some buildings. Many classes were canceled. I was happy about that. I preferred to study by myself in the library. But later, students were removed by the police, and the school was locked down. I went to a public library to study Buddhist psychology. I was determined not to participate in the groups. I didn't trust any of the parties. I was skeptical of almost everything.

When I read Sawaki Roshi and Uchiyama Roshi, I found support for my decision. Part of me felt guilty about not participating in the social movements. However, another part thought that quietly studying Buddhist teaching and practicing zazen was the best way to engage in the world.

13

The Fashion of the Day

KODO SAWAKI:
Kids always want to do what other kids do. When their friends eat a sweet potato, they want to eat a sweet potato. When others eat a certain kind of candy, they want it. When many kids have a bamboo whistle, they ask their parents, "Please buy me a whistle." And not only kids do this.

KOSHO UCHIYAMA:
When the plastic doll Dakkochan was in fashion, I read a letter in the readers' column of a newspaper. It said, "My daughter wanted a Dakkochan, so we went to buy one at a department store. She was very excited. But we had to stand in line, and they sold out while we were waiting. She was extremely disappointed, and I felt sorry for her. Please produce more dolls so everyone can get one."

The mother seemed to be complaining, almost crying. This ridiculous letter made such an impression on me that I still remember its exact words. I think this is a very interesting example of the jumble of blind parental love and group stupidity. Dakkochan dolls would go out of fashion in less than six months or so, and no one would pay any attention to them anymore. Still the mother despaired when her daughter missed the fad.

Similarly, parents think that in order to send their children to a first-class elementary school, they have to enroll them in a first-class kindergarten. So they stand in line for admission. Fanatical mothers want their kids to play piano simply because other children do, without considering their children's ability or interest. So they borrow money to buy a piano. And they pursue other trends, such as the latest cameras, automobiles, air conditioners, etc. Many people find the meaning of their lives in keeping up with fads. As Sawaki Roshi said, not only kids do this. I'd like to say, "Grow up a little."

SHOHAKU OKUMURA:
Sawaki Roshi's first comment here is probably about kids not long after World War II. Today's children aren't interested in such things; they don't know about the bamboo whistle. Desires have changed along with our economic conditions. However, our drive to acquire fashionable things whether or not we really need or like them hasn't changed.

Dakkochan was a cheap plastic doll that children could carry while walking. It was popular among young girls in 1960. More than two million were sold, but the boom lasted less than a year. That was six years before Uchiyama Roshi wrote this article, yet he still remembered the mother's letter to the newspaper.

In the second half of the 1950s, the Japanese media coined the tagline "the three sacred treasures," referring to the most popular electronic appliances: televisions, washing machines, and refrigerators. This was about ten years after the end of World War II, when the Japanese economy began to grow, restoring prosperity. The media inflamed people's desires to buy goods.

Ten years later, in the mid-sixties when Uchiyama Roshi wrote this article, the color TV, air conditioner, and automobile were called the new three sacred treasures. The Japanese economy kept growing. The Tokyo Olympics took place in 1964. The highway between Tokyo and Osaka, as well as the bullet train, were constructed. In 1968, Japan became the second greatest economic power in terms of gross national product.

I lived in a small town, Ibaraki, between Kyoto and Osaka. In the early fifties, the population of Ibaraki was about thirty thousand: the minimum for a town to be designated a city. By 1970, it had grown ten times. When I was a kid, Ibaraki had many rice fields and farms. We could swim in the river until I was around ten. Then swimming was prohibited because a paper factory had been built and the water was polluted. A lot of farmland was destroyed for houses and factories.

To build the highway, we lost our playground. People called these changes "development," which implies that things are getting better, but I felt it was destruction.

Japan became a rich country. People worked hard to make money and buy things. Meanwhile, Uchiyama Roshi was sitting zazen and supporting his practice by begging. To him, it looked like people were manipulated into working to make money, their desires for an ever-higher level of consumption stimulated by the government, big corporations, and media. It seems the same thing is currently happening in many countries. Is this really "development"? This is a very important question.

14.

Dazzled by the Multitude

KODO SAWAKI:
When religious groups attract crowds and build elaborate structures, many people begin to believe these institutions are true religions.

The genuineness of a religion does not depend on how many believers it has. Large numbers are not significant; more people are deluded than aren't. And viruses must outnumber human beings.

These days, people try to accomplish things by forming groups and outnumbering the opposition. But in any group, members are infected with group stupidity. Forming factions within the group and competing with other subgroups is a good example of group paralysis. To be free of group paralysis and become the self that is only the self is the practice of zazen.

KOSHO UCHIYAMA:
No matter how many coal cinders accumulate, they're nothing more than coal cinders. But when a huge amount of something is piled up before them, people are impressed by the sheer volume and think it must amount to something significant.

Blinded by quantity, people cannot perceive quality. Some people, understanding this mob psychology, take advantage of it and think, "Let's establish an organization, build a spectacular temple, and become rich and powerful." Sawaki Roshi walked by himself his entire life, without having any religious organization such as a temple. And yet his sayings influenced many people. I think he lived a magnificent and dignified life.

A genuine religion is not something that aims to establish a large organization by catering to the human desires to make money, attain social position, or avoid illness. To lead a life based on genuine religious insight is to deeply examine the truth of human life, realize it within oneself, and live it moment by moment. Even if something mistakenly referred to as religion spreads everywhere by flattering the desires of the masses, it can't be called a true religion. It's simply a malicious cult ravaging the world like an epidemic. On the other hand, a religion that sincerely examines human ideals and shows us how to realize them can be called a world religion even if only one, or half a person, devotes their life to it.

SHOHAKU OKUMURA:
Another phenomenon in Japan after World War II was the rise of various new religions. The post-war social chaos confused people mentally and spiritually. These new religions took advantage of such conditions. Some were aggressive in converting people, collecting huge amounts of money and constructing spectacular temples. A few religions became active in politics.

Sawaki Roshi and Uchiyama Roshi criticized not only the traditional Buddhist institutions that had lost their vitality like withered old trees but also the new movements that enticed people with promises of wealth, success, and good health. They were another symptom of a society in which people stop thinking for themselves.

15.

Opinions Gone to Seed

KODO SAWAKI:
Some opinions have passed their prime and lost relevance. For instance, when grownups lecture children, they often simply repeat ready-made opinions. They merely say, "Good is good; bad is bad." When greens go to seed, they become hard and fibrous. They aren't edible anymore. We should always see things with fresh eyes!

Often people say, "This is valuable!" But what's really valuable? Nothing. When you die, you have to leave everything behind. Even the national treasures in Kyoto and Nara will sooner or later perish. It's not a problem even if they all burn down.

KOSHO UCHIYAMA:
Often people say of books by famous scholars, "That's a good book. Have you read it?" But when I ask if they understood the book, they say no. We Japanese seem to have an excess of humility. When we read something by a well-known academic, we believe it must be good. If we can't understand it, we think that's our own fault.

Right after World War II, people lined up all night at bookstores to buy a copy of the philosophical work of Professor Kitaro Nishida, as if it were the latest toy. But these books were written in a typically awkward style. People must have opened the books, closed them quickly, and decided they were great because they couldn't be understood.

KODO SAWAKI:
What was the purpose of constructing Kinkakuji, Horyuji, and other old temples? None of them was built for monks to practice Bud-

dhism. They were built only to feed lazy, feckless monks. Therefore, it's no surprise there are monks who set fire to Kinkakuji or Enryakuji. Ginkakuji is the same.

SHOHAKU OKUMURA:
Kitaro Nishida (1870–1945) was a professor at Kyoto University and an important philosopher of the Kyoto school. A friend of D. T. Suzuki, he combined his Zen Buddhist practice with the logic of Western philosophy. Although his books were difficult, his philosophy was popular after the war. Some critics said that his expression "absolutely contradictory self-identity" was almost worshiped as a religious teaching, without being clearly understood.

Kinkakuji, or the Temple of the Golden Pavilion, was burned in 1950 by a young monk. Enryakuji was set afire in the sixteenth century by Oda Nobunaga, a feudal lord attempting to unify the warring states of Japan.

People assume ancient Buddhist temples are precious, but from Sawaki Roshi's point of view, they have nothing to do with the Dharma, so they're useless. He studied Yogacara teachings at Horyuji in Nara for several years, so he knew how monks lived there. As such temples became popular for sightseeing, many people enjoyed the buildings, gardens, paintings, and statues as art. The temples became like museums, and monks turned into administrators. Upper-class monks at these temples grew rich and lived luxuriously.

This opinion was not only Sawaki Roshi's. Dogen Zenji wrote in *Shobogenzo Gyoji*:

> Even if we don't have lofty temple buildings, if we practice, this place can be called a dojo of ancient buddhas. Foolish people in this degenerate age should not be vainly engaged in construction of temple buildings. The buddhas and ancestors never had desires for buildings. Many people today meaninglessly construct a Buddha hall or other temple buildings although they haven't yet clarified the eye of their own self. Such people build temples, not in order to offer the buildings to buddhas, but to make their own houses of fame and profit.

I was raised in Osaka, near Kyoto and Nara. When young, I often visited the old temples there. I liked to walk in the beautiful and peaceful neighborhoods of those temples and look at the Buddhist statues. But after I read this comment by Sawaki Roshi, I lost interest in temples and Buddhist art for many years.

Dogen Zenji and Sawaki Roshi pointed out that these objects were originally made to gratify powerful people's desires for fame and profit, fulfill their vanity, or appease their fear of death. I agree with this criticism. And yet a few days after the earthquake and nuclear disaster in Tohoku on March 11, 2011, I had a chance to visit the temples in Nara. Then I felt how fortunate it was that the Buddha statues, which have silently witnessed Japanese people's suffering and happiness for more than a thousand years, are still there, unburned.

16.

Loyalty

KODO SAWAKI:

When Hojo's troops attacked Kusunoki Masashige's Chihaya fortress, many warriors of the Hojo clan died. It's said they were praised by their friends for meeting "glorious deaths" on the battlefield. Someone composed a poem about the event:

> A man lays down his life in vain for the sake of fame.
> Why doesn't he give up clinging to life for the sake of
>   Dharma?

With the victories of the Sino-Japanese War (1894–95) and the Russo-Japanese War (1904–5), we thought we enlarged Japanese territory. Later we annexed Korea. But when we lost World War II, we lost everything and truly understood that we had only incurred the enmity of people in those countries.

People often talk about loyalty, but I wonder if they know the direction of their loyalty and actions. I myself was a soldier during the Russo-Japanese War and fought hard on the battlefield. But since we lost World War II, and what we thought we had gained was taken away, I can clearly see that what we did was meaningless. There is absolutely no need to wage war.

KOSHO UCHIYAMA:

Sawaki Roshi fought in the Russo-Japanese War and was almost killed. He was a brave warrior who received the Order of the Golden Kite. His statements here are not about other people; they're a reflection on himself. Not only Sawaki Roshi but all Japanese educated before World War II were taught that Japan was the greatest country in the world, ruled by an unbroken line of emperors and absolutely righteous in all its actions, and that we would gain personal immortality if we were faithful to our nation and died for our emperor. This was called "State Shinto," and we believed it.

After World War II, we found what we had been taught wasn't true, and many Japanese reacted against patriotism. I think this is natural. When we reflect on the past and the future, we should question not only loyalty to our country but also loyalty to other countries: the U.S., China, Russia. Whichever country we're devoted to, eventually our actions will be only a page in the book of history. A Japanese proverb says, "If the troops win, their side is called loyal; if the troops lose, their side is called rebel." The important thing is to have a clear-eyed view of the self and to behave sanely and soberly.

KODO SAWAKI:
What is the true self? It's brilliantly transparent like the deep blue sky, and there's no gap between it and all living beings.

SHOHAKU OKUMURA:
In 1332, Kusunoki Masashige fought at Chihaya against Hojo troops who had many more soldiers. This was one of the battles between Emperor Godaigo and the Kamakura Shogunate government, for which Hojo was the regent. The emperor regained political power from Kamakura, but his reign lasted only two-and-a-half years. From the seventeenth century to the end of World War II, Masashige was considered the loyalist and Hojo the rebel from the perspective of the imperial system. But Sawaki Roshi commented that among the Hojo, soldiers killed in battle were praised for their deaths. From Hojo's perspective, the soldiers were loyal. Which side is which? The evaluation depends simply on who wins.

After World War II, the reckoning completely changed. People formerly considered heroes became war criminals. Japanese people became critical of nationalism. During the Cold War, the Japanese were divided into two sides. Right-wingers spoke on behalf of the U.S. and its allies, while left-wingers were loyal to communist countries such as the Soviet Union and China. This is the situation Uchiyama Roshi speaks of. To him, it seemed many people didn't think for themselves but became pawns of someone with greater power.

From his sayings, we can see that Sawaki Roshi was conditioned as a Japanese living in the Meiji, Taisho, and Showa eras—from the end of the nineteenth to the twentieth century. Even though he had no desire for personal fame and profit, he was not free of the views of his time, especially the State Shinto fabricated by the Meiji government. *Shinto*, which literally means "way of the gods," was originally a Japanese folk religion that worshiped everything in nature. After the opening of Japan to the West in 1853, the Japanese government felt that unless Japan achieved economic and military power, it would become a colony of the West, as were other Asian countries at the time. State Shinto was created to give the Japanese people motivation to work hard and even die for their government.

Within the world of "might is right," how can we live as the true self without division between us and others?

17.

Mistaking Technological Advancement for Human Transformation

KODO SAWAKI:
After all our efforts, racking our brains as intensely as possible, we have come to a deadlock. Human beings are idiots. We set ourselves up as wise and then do foolish things.

In spite of our scientific advancement, we haven't yet achieved greatness of character. What's the reason for this?

Since the dawn of history, human beings have constantly fought. No matter how big a war might be, the root cause of it is our minds, which make us live a cat-and-dog life.

We should not forget that modern scientific culture has developed on the basis of our lowest consciousness.

People always talk about "civilization," but civilization and culture are nothing but the collective elaboration of illusory desires. No matter how many wrinkles of illusory desire we have in our brains, from the Buddhist point of view, they will never amount to meaningful advancement for human beings. "Advancement" is the talk of the world, but in what direction are we advancing?

KOSHO UCHIYAMA:
When Sawaki Roshi's term "group stupidity" is directed at our modern civilization, it becomes a criticism of the core of this society. People today are dazzled by advances in science and technology and take human progress to be identical with scientific discovery. This is the fundamental group stupidity of our modern times. We must clearly distinguish between scientific advancement and human progress.

The historian Arnold Toynbee said, "Our modern scientific culture has increased the speed of Adam's original sin with explosive energy. That is all. And we have never released ourselves from original sin." Real human advancement would liberate us from our lowest consciousness, which says, "I want to gain everything without working hard. To do that, I'm ready to fight."

SHOHAKU OKUMURA:

Until I became a teenager in the 1960s, the basic message I received from school and Japanese society in general was that all the suffering and devastation of history were caused by ignorance, and the world was improving because of developments in science and technology. When science reaches its ultimate stage, all our problems will be solved. To achieve this, we need to study hard and gain knowledge.

By the time I was in high school, it became clear that the development of knowledge and technology alone doesn't make the world a better place, particularly when such development is driven by self-centered desire and competitive mind. In Saddhatissa's translation of the Sutta Nipata, one of the oldest Buddhist scriptures, someone asks Shakyamuni Buddha, "Whenever there are arguments and quarrels, there are tears and anguish, arrogance and pride, and grudges and insults to go with them. Can you explain how these things come about? Where do they come from?"

I think this question is still relevant. If Buddha returned to this world, he would be surprised at how much it has changed technologically. In his time, people believed that through diligent practice of meditation they could attain supernatural powers, such as the freedom to travel anywhere and see and hear anything, no matter how far away. Today, thanks to airplanes and the internet, even a child can do these things. But Buddha might also be surprised at how little human nature has transformed. He might think our situation in the twenty-first century is like the story in the Lotus Sutra: While a father was out, his children were playing in the burning house of samsara. When he returned, he called to them to escape the house, but they were so enjoying their toys that they didn't want to leave. Today these children are playing with nuclear power and all the other dangerous toys in our burning house of samsara.

18.

Tunnel Vision

KODO SAWAKI:
The karmic consciousnesses of human beings are not the same. Each of us has our own limited view.

We each see the world only through our particular tunnel. Because we interact while holding our own way of viewing, thinking, and doing, friction occurs in the world.

KOSHO UCHIYAMA:
Usually we think we are most important, and we believe our thoughts are the most reliable yardstick for judging. We use this stick to gauge circumstances and other people's actions. When their behavior or the situation is not in accord with our standards, we get angry, have conflicts, and are troubled.

When we're in this condition, we should use the wisdom that sees this world doesn't exist only for us, our own perspective is not absolutely right, and it's natural that things don't go as we expect. Then we'll be able to breathe more freely and prevent ourselves from causing needless trouble with others.

For example, if a mother thinks her daughter-in-law is awful because she never does things the way the mother-in-law expects, conflict is unavoidable. But if the mother-in-law thinks it's quite natural that her daughter-in-law has her own way of doing things, she can find peace of mind. And if the daughter-in-law does even one thing as the mother expects, this is rare and wonderful. If they have the same attitude about this, both women can appreciate and cooperate with each other.

Prince Shotoku expressed it skillfully. He said, "Simply, we are all ordinary human beings." Not only are others foolish, ordinary beings, but we ourselves are as well.

SHOHAKU OKUMURA:

Prince Shotoku (574–622 CE) was the crown prince and regent of his aunt, Empress Suiko, who reigned from 593–628. He made efforts to adopt Chinese culture to make Japan a more civilized country in politics, culture, religion, and the arts. He helped Buddhism flourish, establishing temples such as Shitennoji in Osaka, and Hokoji and Horyuji in Nara. It's said that he wrote commentaries on the three most important Mahayana sutras: the Lotus, Vimalakirti, and Queen Srimala sutras. Here Uchiyama Roshi refers to article 10 of the seventeen-article constitution attributed to Prince Shotoku. I think this article serves well as a commentary on Sawaki Roshi's and Uchiyama Roshi's discussion:

> Cut off your anger and cast aside your resentful expressions. Do not be angry even when others are different from us. All people have minds. And the mind of each person has its own preferences. When they consider something right, we consider the same thing wrong. When we consider something right, they consider the same thing wrong. We are not necessarily sages, and they are not necessarily fools. All of us are simply ordinary human beings. Who can set up absolutely correct criteria to judge right from wrong? We are all wise and foolish in some ways. There is no time we can conclude who is wiser and who is more foolish, just as a circle has no end. For this reason, when others become angry, we should be mindful of our own faults.

Uchiyama Roshi's discussion of a mother and daughter-in-law is a classic example of twisted human relationships within the structure of the traditional Japanese family, in which at least three generations lived together. After Uchiyama Roshi gave a Dharma talk on this topic, a mother-in-law said to him, "Thank you very much for your

wonderful talk. It should be a great lesson for my daughter-in-law."
The daughter-in-law said, "I hope my mother-in-law understood
what you said." Because the majority of Japanese families today are
nuclear families, this example isn't so relevant anymore. However,
similar problems occur in any human community.

19

Gathering Food and Hatching Eggs

KODO SAWAKI:

Because people steep themselves in their own lives, they blindly believe there must be something especially important in their activities. But actually, the life of human beings is not so different from a swallow's: the males collect food, the females hatch eggs.

KOSHO UCHIYAMA:

This is the season swallows are flying. People working in the shadows of tall buildings in the city probably spend the springtime without seeing swallows hatching. It's a lovely sight.

Even when Sawaki Roshi bluntly criticized how people live, he usually used humorous expressions and said he was smiling inside.

The majority of people just get by, living day to day, never seeing their lives as a whole. Kobo Daishi called this *ishoteiyoshin*, the mind of the lowly man, goatish in its desires.

KODO SAWAKI:

Just because we become a bride or bridegroom, this doesn't mean we automatically get a clear view of our lives. Life is still full of questions. Yet when a foolish man who doesn't understand life marries a foolish woman who doesn't understand life, everyone says, "Congratulations!" This is most incomprehensible to me.

When I visited Manchuria, I saw people using big dogs to pull carts. A person would ride in the cart dangling meat on the end of a fishing rod before the dog's nose. Although the dogs pulled the carts with all their might, trying to get a bite of meat, they couldn't. When they reached their destination, the meat was finally given to them. They ate it in one gulp. Most people are like those dogs. Every month, they chase the paycheck that hangs before their eyes. On payday, they gulp it down. Then they begin to run after the next.

SHOHAKU OKUMURA:
While the societal roles of men and women are changing and becoming more collaborative, the necessary activities of providing food and raising children are not different from a swallow's way of life.

Kobo Daishi is the honorific title given by the emperor to Kukai (774–835), founder of the Shingon school, the Japanese version of Vajrayana Buddhism. Kukai was one of the greatest masters in the history of Japanese Buddhism. In his *Jujushinron*, or *The Ten Stages of the Development of Minds*, and the shorter version of the same text, *Hizohoyaku*, or *The Precious Key to the Secret Treasury*, Kukai described the development of the human mind in ten stages; Uchiyama Roshi refers to the first and lowest stage. *Goatish mind* comes from the Mahavairocana Sutra, one of the main Vajrayana sutras. Yoshito Hakeda offers the following translation of Kukai's words:

> What is meant by this mind? It is the name given to the lowly man who, in his madness, does not distinguish between good and evil, and who, ignorant like a stupid child, does not believe in the law of cause and effect. The lowly man creates karma and receives its fruits; he receives then a thousand different forms of life in the process of transmigration. His ignorance, therefore, can be compared to that of a goat.

According to Kukai, people with this type of mind live driven by desire for food, clothes, sex, fame, and wealth, working day and night, creating good and bad karma, and transmigrating in the six realms of samsara. He also wrote about family relationships based on this goatish mind.

> Although children and parents may love each other, they do not know the character of their love. Although husband

and wife may love each other, they do not know the nature of their love. Their love is like a flowing stream whose water changes perpetually, or like the sparks of a flame. They are bound by the rope of deluded thoughts and are intoxicated by the wine of ignorance.

If family connections are based only on this goatish mind, it's natural for family life to become a kind of samsara that can easily be troubled or destroyed—love becoming hatred. We need to develop our minds to understand who we truly are, who others are, and that we are all equal, ordinary beings.

The majority of people Sawaki Roshi encountered in his childhood with his adoptive parents lived with this goatish mind. He didn't want to live that way and so left home to become a monk. Although he left that life in muddy water, he never disparaged or hated those people. Even in his criticism, we can see his warmth and compassion. He supported his adoptive parents until the end of their lives and said to his father, "You are my good teacher. Because of your example, I cannot let myself stop practicing and become corrupt."

20.

A Depressed Look

KODO SAWAKI:
It's silly to complain with a depressed face: "I have no money, it's hard to make a living, I have so many debts," etc. People with a starvation mentality always desire to be more fortunate. That's why they're constantly craving something and complaining about their current conditions.

Even when they're not going hungry, people complain about not having enough money. This attitude causes an imaginary hunger, a self-created nightmare that makes people cry out. Words alone can cause great trouble.

Even a beggar laughs sometimes, and even a millionaire cries. Money is not a big deal.

KOSHO UCHIYAMA:
Seven or eight years ago at twilight a man about thirty came to Antaiji with a sad look and said, "I have nothing to eat." A porridge of rice and vegetables was just ready, so I invited him to join us for dinner, saying, "If you're hungry, first please eat with us. We can talk afterward." Then he said something strange: "I have nothing to eat, but I'm not really hungry now."

When I talked with him after dinner, I learned he was living with his wife and mother and had a job. Although the company he worked for wasn't one of the biggest, still he had some income and was certainly not starving. I told him, "Don't say this nonsense that you have nothing to eat when you're not even hungry! You should rather say that your income is not enough to satisfy your vanity."

He stayed and practiced with us for about a week. On leaving, he said happily, "My life at home is better than your life here." Our temple life must have looked shabby to him. But I felt good because our poverty enabled him to appreciate his own life. Unless you're really hungry, it's better not to indulge in a depressed look. You'll be happier.

SHOHAKU OKUMURA:

Uchiyama Roshi is playing with words here. The Japanese expression *kuenai* means both "I have nothing to eat" and "It's hard to make a living." I'm not sure whether Uchiyama Roshi really thought this man was starving, or if he understood what the man meant and was making fun of him from the beginning.

Since the time of Shakyamuni Buddha, poverty has never been shameful for monks. They renounced wealth and privilege, keeping only one begging bowl and three robes. Dogen Zenji also emphasized intentional poverty. In *Shobogenzo Zuimonki*, he often talked about this. For example, when asked by a monk what to keep in mind while studying the way, he answered, "First of all, a person studying the Way should be poor. If you possess great wealth, you will definitely lose aspiration." He also said, "Being poor is being intimate with the Way."

On another occasion he observed, "I have spent more than ten years without any possessions and I have never worried about how to obtain them. To think of accumulating even a little bit of wealth is a great obstacle. Without thinking of how to gain or store up things you will naturally receive as much as you need to stay alive for a while. Each person has his allotted share; heaven and earth bestow it on us. Even though you don't run around seeking it, you will receive it without fail."

Of course, voluntary poverty was the teaching for monks, for home leavers. The Buddha taught laypeople to work diligently and honestly and then share their wealth as their practice of generosity, which is known as *dana paramita*. Of course, depending on their situation, laypeople cannot always be successful and rich. For those in poverty, the monks' way of life without desire for wealth can be an inspiration, as Uchiyama Roshi's lifestyle was to the man with the depressed look.

It's interesting that in modern times we often complain about the many things we lack, and we consider this normal. But when people appear satisfied and happy with their lives, we think there's something wrong with them—they lack ambition or are lazy—and we consider their lives to be a kind of failure. If we're ambitious and desire to become rich and cannot do so, that's a failure. But if we have no such desire, there can be neither failure nor success.

21

Calculating the Difference

KODO SAWAKI:
During World War II, when I visited a coal mine in Kyushu, they allowed me to go into the mine. Like the miners, I put on a hard hat with a headlamp and went down the shaft in an elevator. For a while, I thought the elevator was going down very fast. Then I started to feel as if it were going up. I shone my headlamp on the shaft and realized the elevator was still going down steadily. When an elevator starts descending with increasing speed, we feel it going down, but once the speed becomes fixed, we feel as if the elevator were rising. The balance has shifted. In the ups and downs of life, we're deceived by the difference in the balance.

Saying, "I've had satori!" is only feeling a difference in the balance. Saying, "I'm deluded!" is feeling another. To say food tastes delicious or terrible, to be rich or poor, all are just feelings about shifts in the balance.

In most cases, our ordinary way of thinking only considers differences in the balance.

Human beings put *I* into everything without knowing it. We sometimes say, "That was really good!" What's it good for? It's just good for *me*, that's all.

We usually do things expecting some personal profit. And if the results turn out different from our hidden agenda, we feel disappointed and exhausted.

KOSHO UCHIYAMA:

Good or bad luck is always our main concern. But in reality, is there good or bad fortune? There isn't. There are only calculations using our expectations as a yardstick. Precisely because we expect to make things profitable for ourselves, we regret when they aren't. Only because we compete with others do we experience as defeat the difference between our expectations and reality.

True religion has nothing to do with human desire for profit or calculating measurements between expectations and events. It's human to have expectations, but clinging to them causes suffering. If we can loosen our grip on expectations and settle down on whichever side of the balance we fall at this moment, we find unshakable peace of mind, and a truly stable life unfolds. Doing zazen is ceasing to be a person always gauging gain and loss and evaluating life according to such calculations. To practice zazen is to stop being an ordinary human being.

SHOHAKU OKUMURA:

We human beings have the ability to think of things not in front of us.

We create stories in our minds in which the hero or heroine is always us. We evaluate what happened in the past, we analyze our present conditions, and we anticipate what should happen in the future. This is an important ability. Because of it, we can create art, study history, and have visions of the future. Without it, we couldn't write or enjoy poems or movies. Almost all of human culture depends on seeing things not in front of our eyes.

This means almost all culture is fictitious. Our ability to create such fictions is the reality of our lives. We cannot live without it. But this ability leads to many problems. We have certain expectations of our stories. If things go as we expect, we feel like heavenly beings, but if not, we feel we're in hell. Often we desire more and more without ever experiencing satisfaction, like hungry ghosts.

It's important to see that it's not life that causes suffering but our expectation that life should be the way we want. We can't live without expectation, but if we can handle the feelings caused by the difference between our expectations and reality, that's liberation.

Zazen practice as taught by Dogen Zenji, Sawaki Roshi, and Uchi-yama Roshi is taking a break from watching the screen of our stories and sitting down on the ground of the reality that exists before our imagination. When we're not taken in by our fictitious world, we can enjoy and learn from the stories we make.

22.

Religion Is Life

KODO SAWAKI:
How we live our everyday lives has to be the main concern of religion.

KOSHO UCHIYAMA:
On television, it's permissable to show scenes of explicit sex and crimes, including murder. Big posters of nude women can be posted on the street. Although kids see these TV shows and posters, not many people worry about this. At the same time, it's illegal to teach religion in public school. To me this is one of the mysteries of twentieth-century Japan.

Maybe people think that "religion" means established sects, superstition, or fanaticism. It's certainly true that if an innocent child is influenced by one-sided, fixed doctrines, this will lead to great problems. So one might say it's understandable that the government bans religious education in public schools. On the other hand, if religion means teachings about the most important matter of our lives—how we should live—then we should worry about the next generation, growing up in a society without any religious education, yet constantly confronted with images of sex and violence. If things continue like this, we'll find young people becoming more and more destructive.

I hope the time will come for religion to be taught in school without indoctrination, but as a lesson about the most important question of life: how to live.

KODO SAWAKI:

"Religion" is to live out the ever fresh self, which is not deceived by anything.

Religion must not be a system of dogma. Religion is life. Religion has to function as life. Worshiping sutras is not enough. Religion must manifest itself freely and inexhaustibly in all activities of life, everywhere and always.

SHOHAKU OKUMURA:

When the government supported religious institutions and forced people to adopt them, this caused terrible problems. An example is the State Shinto from the Meiji era to the end of World War II. When political power and religious authority are combined, there can be no freedom. I don't think that's what Uchiyama Roshi is recommending.

As I mentioned in chapter 2, the Japanese equivalent of the word "religion" is *shukyo*. This word originally referred to Buddhism: the teaching, or *kyo*, about fundamental reality, or *shu*. Sawaki Roshi and Uchiyama Roshi used the word "religion" to mean awakening to reality, rather than a system of belief and worship within a particular tradition.

Uchiyama Roshi thought the most important questions of our life should be taught in schools as the subject "Human Life." He even wrote a textbook as an example. In that book he remarked:

> When the time comes to teach "Human Life" in schools, I think the word "religion" should be eliminated. When we use the word in its traditional meaning . . . a strange atmosphere is created. This is because traditional religions always set up some authority beyond our understanding and force people to believe certain myths and doctrines. And yet in our life as the self that is born and dies naked, fundamentally no such authority and belief are necessary. We just need to straightforwardly see the reality of life as the self and teach how to live based on that reality.

Uchiyama Roshi's searching, studying, and practicing were ways to study the "self." He wasn't interested in becoming a believer of a traditional religion. In his search for truth, he found some people in the Buddhist tradition who had the same attitude. One was the Buddha, who said, "The self is the only foundation of the self." Another was Dogen, who said, "To study the Buddha way is to study the self." Sawaki Roshi emphasized zazen practice as "the self selfing the self." Throughout his life, Uchiyama Roshi continued to read the Bible as one of the ways to study the self. In his final days, he said, "I am neither a Buddhist nor a Christian. I am just who I am."

23

Our Lives of Inertia

KODO SAWAKI:
Human beings are strange. Although we have an intelligent look, we are simply groping in darkness.

Human beings work diligently merely to avoid boredom.

There are too many things that attract us in this world. We want to do this and that. But once we experience or get these things, we find they're nothing important.

There are people who never discover their own true way of life.

KOSHO UCHIYAMA:
If I broach the subject of the meaning of our lives, or what makes us feel life is worth living, you might think I'm being preachy. But when we reflect deeply on our lives, we realize this isn't an academic question; our accustomed ways of life lack vitality.

We get up in the morning merely by force of habit, eat breakfast by force of habit, go to work by force of habit, meet people by force of habit, watch television by force of habit, and read magazines by force of habit. We spend most of our time in inertia.

However, if we ask ourselves whether we live with meaning, most people would answer "yes." Why do we feel our lives are worth living? We're always running after one thing or another so we can avoid deeply considering this question. When we play games, we find the significance of life in winning. When we go to a department store, we find the meaning of life in shopping. If we can't afford certain things, we find meaning in the fantasy that someday we'll be rich. When we watch sports on TV, we find the meaning of life in hoping our favorite athletes will win. These activities are merely diversions of the moment.

No matter how noisy the modern world in which we live, I hope we can sincerely reflect on the meaning of our lives as a whole, instead of living by inertia.

SHOHAKU OKUMURA:

The expression "groping in darkness" can be used with a positive connotation, as in Yunyan and Daowu's discussion of the thousand hands and eyes of Avalokiteshvara; Yuanyan asks how the bodhisattva can use so many hands and eyes, and Daowu replies that it's as natural as adjusting your pillow in the middle of the night. In *Shobogenzo Kannon*, Dogen explains this phrase as intimate actions without separation or discrimination between subject and object.

Here Sawaki Roshi uses the expression with a negative meaning: we don't know the direction of our lives as a whole, even though we're advanced in intellect and have so much knowledge. We pursue things we believe will give us happiness, such as toys, boyfriends or girlfriends, credentials, jobs, money, and so on, depending on the stage of our lives.

We fumble for whatever looks attractive and exciting at the time, but we don't think about our overall direction. In Mahayana Buddhism, practitioners take the four bodhisattva vows as our life's direction. These vows are endless; they can never be completely fulfilled. Based on these general vows, we also take particular vows we wish to accomplish within this life, depending on our characters and capabilities. Every day we make the effort to take even one step toward fulfilling our vows.

A bodhisattva vow is not a goal but a direction. The important point is to live mindfully, led by vow rather than personal desire.

24

The Money Solution

KODO SAWAKI:
If we have no money, we're in trouble. But it's good to know there are more important things than money. If we have no sexual desire, something might be wrong, but it's good to know there are more important things than sexual desire.

KOSHO UCHIYAMA:
If I were very rich, I'd buy everything. If I gave people money, they'd greet me with smiles. I could live in those smiles. When someone is in trouble, often they're suffering from a shortage of cash. I'd give money unstintingly and solve people's problems. If I got sick, I'd go to one of those hospitals furnished like a luxury hotel and hire beautiful young nurses. I could receive medical treatment while feasting my eyes. When I got old, I could have people thinking I was kind and trustworthy. I could enjoy a fabulous second youth. I'd act as a peacemaker, saying, "Hey, I'll buy the war!" and resolve conflicts by giving each side a fat check.

There are always disagreements in economics and ideology. Although they seem complicated, most problems can be solved with money, if we have enough. And yet there's at least one thing that cannot be fixed this way: the belief that *all* problems can be solved with money. If you believe that money can answer any question, you become totally dependent on it. And unfortunately, this difficulty cannot be solved with money. This is a real problem.

Once I met a man who had inherited a large fortune from his parents but was so worried about losing it that he became neurotic. We read that in Sweden many people commit suicide out of despair, even though the country takes care of its citizens. When people look into themselves, they don't find their lives to be at all settled.

Here we find the difference between solution through money and liberation through religion.

SHOHAKU OKUMURA:
In the mid-1960s, when Uchiyama Roshi wrote these articles, Japan was still poor, but people were working very hard to establish prosperity. Around the same time, I was taught that Sweden was the most developed country in terms of social welfare. Although people pay high taxes, the government supplies necessities to all citizens throughout their lives. And yet relatively many people there commit suicide. I concluded that a well-developed system of social welfare doesn't necessarily make people happy.

However, during the last several years, I've had the chance to visit Sweden three times. Because of my impressions there, I wondered about the truth of what I had been taught. So I researched online the national suicide rates from 1900 to 2010. From after World War II until its economic boom, Japan had the highest suicide rate in the world. But from the 1960s to 1980s, when the Japanese economy was strong, the rate decreased significantly. And after the mid-1990s, when the economy declined, the suicide rate again rose sharply. Now Japan has the fifth highest suicide rate in the world and Sweden is twenty-ninth. Since the four countries above Japan are all relatively small, it's possible Japan has the largest number of people who commit suicide.

It's true that in 1966, when Uchiyama Roshi wrote this article, the suicide rate in Sweden was higher than in Japan. Some contemporary Japanese scholars explain this by citing the fact that in Sweden from 1960 to 1970, many women started to work outside the home. They argue that the traditional family system was damaged, and this is one of the reasons for the increased suicide rate. Sweden also experienced a high rate of divorce and crime around the same time. These scholars contend that because of the development of the social welfare system, the suicide rate later declined.

If this sociological explanation is true, then what Uchiyama Roshi said above is not necessarily correct; the number of suicides does not depend simply on existential problems within rich, financially secure lives—many people commit suicide when nations are in social disorder and economic crisis. So we have to say that economic conditions are important not because we can solve all our problems with money, but because people's attitudes are strongly influenced by such conditions. However, I still believe that finding unshakable stability in our lives independent of financial circumstances is important.

25.

Everyone Is Naked

KODO SAWAKI:
To live in this floating world is to wander from place to place pursuing mere titles. Each of us is born naked. But then we are given a name and registered. We're covered with clothes, a nipple is stuffed into our mouth, and so on. When we grow up people say, "This person is great, strong, clever, rich." We find consolation in words, when in fact everyone is simply naked.

KOSHO UCHIYAMA:
Jean-Jacques Rousseau said, "Even emperors, nobles, and wealthy men were born naked and poor, and at the end of their lives they must die naked and poor." Without a doubt, this is true. For a short while between birth and death, we put on various complicated clothes.

Some wear luxurious garments, some rags, some prison uniforms. There are clothes of status and class, joy and anger, sadness and comfort, delusion and enlightenment. All these are nothing other than clothes.

However, we unwittingly take these clothes to be our real selves and devote ourselves to obtaining by any means even a slightly better wardrobe. As long as we live, we must wear some kind of clothes. I hope that we don't forget our true selves are naked, and without losing sight of this, examine our clothed lives and make necessary adjustments. The Heart Sutra says, "No birth, no extinction, no defilement, no purity." This refers to the true, naked self that has cast off even the clothes called "birth and death" and "enlightenment and delusion."

KODO SAWAKI:

Whether they're beauties or not, when women die, each is the same. A beautiful woman's skull is no better than a plain one's.

There are no rich, no poor, no great, no ordinary. These are only words that appear for a moment like a flash of lightning.

SHOHAKU OKUMURA:

In one of his past lives, Shakyamuni Buddha was a brilliant person named Sumedha. His parents died when he was very young. When he grew old enough to inherit his family's wealth, his guardian showed him what his ancestors had accumulated for six generations: piles of gold, silver, jewels, etc. But Sumedha realized that although his ancestors worked, competed, and fought to acquire these possessions, none could enjoy even a penny after passing away. And he resolved not to maintain the family wealth but to give it to people in need and become a spiritual practitioner. That was the beginning of Shakyamuni's journey toward awakening.

Dogen Zenji said in *Shobogenzo Shukkekudoku* ("The Virtue of Leaving Home"), "When impermanence suddenly arrives, kings, ministers, intimates, servants, spouse, children, and precious treasures cannot help you. We go to the Yellow Spring, the world of the dead, by ourselves. The only things that accompany us are wholesome, unwholesome, or other karmas we have made."

While alive, we have to wear clothes as the conditions of our lives. But we need to understand that one day we'll have to leave our clothing behind. When we die, we give up the clothes we've worn and become our naked selves. The Egyptian emperors who built the pyramids couldn't take them to the other world.

My ancestors were merchants in Osaka for six generations. They accumulated some wealth, but it was lost one night in March 1945 during a bombing by the U.S. My family lost everything three years before I was born. Because of this, my father told me when I was a teenager that since I had nothing to inherit, I could become anything I liked. I feel I was really lucky; because my family lost its wealth, I could become a Buddhist monk.

26.

Seeing the World from a Casket

 **KODO SAWAKI:**

A shower
In the middle of a fight
About irrigation

After a long drought, farmers fight over water for their rice fields. In the middle of the dispute, a shower hits. Since there's no other reason to fight, when it rains the problem disappears. There will be no difference between the beautiful and the plain when they're eighty. The original reality is empty and clear.

KOSHO UCHIYAMA:
"Since there's no other reason to fight, when it rains the problem disappears." I'd like to read this sentence carefully and savor its meaning.

It's quite possible that if I go out now, I may have a car accident that will immediately finish me off. This kind of unexpected death is more likely in modern times than before. If I were run down by a car, all the problems in my thoughts, such as "I want this, I want that"; my frustrated anger, "Oh . . . that fool!"; or my longing for a certain woman would be resolved quite spontaneously, as the argument about irrigation suddenly disappears when it rains.

As long as we're alive, we'll have all different kinds of problems. These troubles are the conditions of being alive. But I believe it's important to take a fresh look at them given the assumption that in the next moment, we might be hit by a car and laid in a coffin. We can open our minds to live in a more leisurely way, knowing that we don't have to get stuck in our self-centered opinions, gritting our teeth and furrowing our brows.

In short, zazen is seeing this world from the casket, without *me*.

KODO SAWAKI:
Imagine looking back on our lives after we die. We'll see that so many things didn't matter.

SHOHAKU OKUMURA:
Sawaki Roshi's expression "the original reality is empty and clear" comes from "Xinxinming," the famous Zen poem attributed to the Third Ancestor of Chinese Zen, Sengcan. The poem begins:

> The supreme Way is without difficulty.
> It only dislikes picking and choosing.
> If there is neither hate nor love,
> It reveals itself empty and clear.

In a severe drought farmers cannot avoid picking and choosing. Their fields are not others'. If they cannot get water, their rice will die, and they'll have no harvest. During droughts in ancient times, there were often fights among villages by the same river, and farmers in the same village, to get even a little more water for their fields. In the midst of the fight, the sky might suddenly darken, and it might start to rain. Then the farmers lost their reason for conflict.

When we soften self-centered discrimination and live without being driven by hatred and love, the supreme way beyond duality manifests itself. And when we see the true interdependent reality of all beings, we can relax and open our clinging minds. Our zazen is to sit in our own caskets and view things from nonduality, or complete interconnectedness.

As all rivers flow into the ocean, when we die we return to oneness. In fact, we always live within this ocean even though we experience our lives as separate. A Japanese poet wrote of rivers flowing within the ocean: river and ocean are both manifestations of the larger circulation of water. Depending on our perspective, we see them as separate or as one.

27

Ghosts and the Power of Suggestion

KODO SAWAKI:

People often ask me, "Do ghosts exist?" Those who think about such matters are ghosts themselves.

KOSHO UCHIYAMA:

Sawaki Roshi always made unequivocal statements. We should understand this saying to be his definition of ghosts. Sawaki Roshi is saying that a ghost cannot exist independently of the human mind, that human beings who entertain the delusion of wondering whether ghosts exist are themselves unreal.

Some people believe psychics who tell them they're haunted by the soul of an ancestor or they can summon the spirits of the dead to solve the problems of the living. Although this is simply a business, when people hear such things, they become frightened, lose their common sense, and are swindled out of money. Those who are influenced by such statements and can't walk their own paths are the real ghosts.

Moreover, people easily affected by the power of suggestion are unreliable. When they get sick and their condition deteriorates, they become depressed and foolish. When they recover and the doctor pronounces them cured, they assume the doctor has given up on them. They can't regain their mental balance because of the suggestion that they're sick. Under such conditions, they can easily be influenced by a charismatic religious leader. After a mesmerizing prayer, incantation, or laying on of hands, they believe they're cured. Those who are easily manipulated are the true phantoms. Such tales have nothing to do with the reality of human life.

KODO SAWAKI:

People sometimes say they saw the spirit of a dead person or dreamed of someone when the person was dying. These are just details in the vast landscape of transmigration within samsara.

SHOHAKU OKUMURA:

The expression "unequivocal statements" at the beginning of Uchiyama Roshi's comment derives from the famous Zen poem "Shodoka," or "The Song of Verification of the Way." In this poem, Yongjia Xuanjue (665–713), a disciple of the Sixth Ancestor, wrote:

> A true monk is recognized by his decisive words
> If you cannot confirm my saying, ask me as you wish.

The translator Jeffrey Broughton offers these words by Bodhidharma:

> It is as if there were someone who painted dragons and tigers with his own hand and yet, upon looking at them, became frightened. Deluded people are also like this. The brush of thought and consciousnesses paints razor mountains and sword forests, and yet it is thought and the consciousnesses that fear them.

Sawaki Roshi's definition of a ghost is someone who paints images in their mind and then is frightened by their own creations. This is how we haunt ourselves. Zazen is a way to awaken from our daydreams and nightmares.

28

In the Family

KODO SAWAKI:
Too often, home is nothing more than a place where husband and wife, parents and children, spoil and constrain each other.

KOSHO UCHIYAMA:
I don't think I'm at all qualified to advise people, especially about family problems. But this world is a strange place. Many people come to me for advice about their families, even though I don't have one. They open their hearts and tell me their troubles quite frankly. I cannot reject such people because sometimes they travel a great distance for this purpose. Probably since this is a temple, they feel safe, trusting that what they say won't leak out to others.

After listening to such people for a number of years, I found an interesting cause-and-effect pattern in their stories. People who have troubles at home often got married only out of mutual sexual attraction. Although they may live together for many years, they never make an effort to form a relationship based on mutual respect. When their sexual passion diminishes, they treat each other like strangers or come to hate each other and let their home fall into chaos. If they want to divorce, they sometimes can't because of the opinions of others, their children, or finances.

Consider the relationship between parents and children. No matter how much they hate each other at times, they are fundamentally similar, and when they lock horns, there can be trouble—passionate mother and passionate daughter, stubborn father and stubborn son, greedy inlaws and greedy young couple, unfeeling parents and unfeeling children. It would be helpful if they could realize they have horns pointing in the same direction and therefore sympathize with one another. If they continually provoke each other and butt heads, it's endless trouble.

To create a home that's truly a place of rest, thoughtfulness, and love, we should respect each other's feelings and opinions, reflect on ourselves, and make an effort to live in harmony. At the very least, home should not be a place where a family criticizes, abuses, or kills each other.

SHOHAKU OKUMURA:
Buddhism was originally a teaching for home leavers, for renunciants. The Buddha himself left his palace and family to seek the spiritual path to liberation. However, from the beginning of Buddhism, householders were part of the Buddhist sangha. Lay Buddhists received five precepts and participated in the monks' practice on full and new moon days. They supported home leavers with offerings of food, medicine, robes, bedding, and so on. Although the majority of the Buddha's teachings were addressed to home leavers, there are some teachings for householders. For example, when he met with a group of husbands and wives, the Buddha taught about marriage. He said there are four kinds of marriage: a wretch lives with a wretch, a wretch lives with a goddess, a god lives with a wretch, and a god lives with a goddess.

In Bhikkhu Bodhi's translation, the Buddha says:

> How does a wretch live with a wretch? Here, householders, the husband is one who destroys life; takes what is not given; engages in sexual misconduct; speaks falsely; and indulges in wines, liquor, and intoxicants, the basis for negligence; he is immoral, of bad character; he dwells at home with a heart obsessed by the stain of stinginess; he abuses and reviles ascetics and Brahmins. And his wife is exactly the same in all respects. It is in such a way that a wretch lives with a wretch.

In the second and third kinds of marriage, one spouse is a wretch but the other is the opposite: a god or goddess. Finally, when both husband and wife are the opposites of what the Buddha describes, they're like a god living with a goddess.

The Buddha recommended that householders keep the five precepts for laypeople: not killing, not stealing, not engaging in sexual misconduct, not speaking falsehood, and not abusing intoxicants. It's interesting that the Buddha called such people "gods" and "goddesses"; people living this way already enjoy heaven in this world.

Sawaki Roshi's adoptive parents could be an example of the first kind of marriage. Uchiyama Roshi's point is that if a husband and wife fail to develop a relationship based on respect, their home can be a hell. Heaven and hell are right here, depending how we live.

29.

What Makes You Attractive?

KODO SAWAKI:
What are we so worried about all the time? If we're not careful, we'll waste our lives chasing after our hopes.

Human beings are simple and childish: we only want to be rich, healthy, and beautiful—that's enough for us.

What have you ever thought about besides how to satisfy your desires for sex and food?

We're always deceived by our bodies and minds, and we're foolish.

KOSHO UCHIYAMA:
I was appalled recently when I overheard a conversation between two middle-aged women who were saying, "A man without money is only half appealing." Probably women say such things because these days they only meet men who are so limited that half their value really is their money. I feel sorry for women who only know men like that. Men should exert themselves to become more than beasts of burden working for money.

But I don't think this restricted view of a person's worth concerns only relations between men and women. I'd like to investigate the fundamental question: what makes a person attractive? If we ask what the other half of a man's appeal is, the answer would probably be potency. So the women's words reflect modern people's view that nothing matters besides money and sex.

But shouldn't both men and women possess more attractiveness than just sexiness and wealth? I think we should have primary appeal as human beings. We should aspire to nurture our excellence as humans, which makes us attractive to each other.

 KODO SAWAKI:
You don't have to save every penny to live well in this world.

SHOHAKU OKUMURA:
When Uchiyama Roshi was a university student, his father's company went bankrupt. He saw many people who used to be loyal and kind to his family suddenly change their attitude. Consequently he resolved to live without worshiping money. In his eighty-six years, he had a regular job and income for only six months, while he taught at a Catholic seminary. He devoted his entire life to searching for and sharing the truth of human life. When I read his book, he was the first person I had encountered who lived with such an attitude. This was his greatest appeal for me. He lived in poverty but his life was extremely rich. In his final days, he wrote a poem:

> Though poor, never poor
> Though sick, never sick
> Though aging, never aging
> Though dying, never dying
> Reality prior to division—
> Herein lies unlimited depth.

I believe that living in a way that expresses this unlimited depth of reality is the true attractiveness of human beings.

30.

One's Own Life

KODO SAWAKI:
It seems that human beings don't wake up unless we're compelled to compete for prizes. We're not ostriches; why must we run races? We're not seals; why the swimming contests? We're not kittens; why scramble for a ball?

KOSHO UCHIYAMA:
Sports are very popular these days, but actually we should say "spectator sports" are popular. Some people watch their favorite athlete's or team's games without fail and make a big deal out of them, though it seems they hardly have time to reflect on their own lives. I wonder about this. If they say it's just entertainment, that's fine. But too much entertainment, like everything else, must be questioned from the perspective of the deepest values and main purpose of one's life.

KODO SAWAKI:
Because they're bored, people kill time by agonizing, falling in love, drinking, reading novels, and watching sports; they do things halfheartedly and incompletely, alienated from their lives, rather than living with determination in a decisive direction. For them life is *ukiyo*, the floating world: a place of floundering and wasting time doing random things.

Everywhere in this world, people go to war from sheer boredom, brandishing deadly weapons as if they were children's toys. Without considering what they're really doing, they simply keep busy. We think such activity must be significant. But actually it isn't. Only the grave waits for us.

Human beings look clever and boast that we're the lords of creation. In fact we don't even know how to take care of ourselves. We kill time watching sports or pursuing other vapid forms of entertainment to avoid facing ourselves. And we justify it by saying everyone else is the same.

When children complain, their parents scold them, saying, "Why don't you understand?" But the parents don't understand either. They're ignorant of the true nature of their own lives.

SHOHAKU OKUMURA:

Shortly after Shakyamuni Buddha attained awakening, he entered a grove and sat under a tree. Soon thirty young men came to picnic nearby with their wives. One of them didn't have a wife, so he brought a courtesan. While they enjoyed themselves, this woman stole their valuables and fled. The men ran around looking for her. As they wandered, they found the Buddha sitting under a tree. They approached him and asked if he had seen the courtesan.

The Buddha asked, "Why are you looking for her?" The young men told him what had happened. Then the Buddha said, "What do you think, young men? Which is better: searching for a woman or searching for the self?" They replied, "It's better to search for the self." The Buddha said, "Then, young men, sit down and I will teach you." After hearing the Buddha's teaching, they became his disciples.

This story appears in the Mahavagga section of the Pali Vinaya. Sawaki Roshi and Uchiyama Roshi are asking the same question here: "Which is better, to go in search of a woman or to go in search of the self?" Instead of seeking meaning and how to live, most people pursue external things to avoid facing themselves and to gain excitement and satisfaction that last only a short while. These days, many people work for money without thinking about the larger meaning of what they're doing. After work they distract themselves from the stress and frustration of their lives with the internet, video games, and TV. Many don't know the purpose or value of their lives.

For example, a schoolteacher might have chosen this career to help children, but under the pressures of large classes, insufficient time, and lack of respect from students and their parents, the teacher might lose sight of their original intention and begin to see the job merely as a way to make money. Then school becomes like an assembly line and the teachers like factory workers.

Although sometimes we cannot escape a system, I think we should make whatever effort we can to improve both our attitude and the system, even in small ways.

31

The Viewpoint of the Ordinary Person

KODO SAWAKI:
In ancient times, people discussed lucky and unlucky directions for almost everything. Directions had a kind of mystical significance. Nowadays, we know that the earth goes around the sun, and we throw toy balloons—satellites—up around the earth. We can't figure out which direction is which anymore.

> In delusion, the three worlds are like a fortress.
> In realization, the ten-direction world is empty.
> Originally there is neither east nor west.
> Where is south or north?

What Master Soseki says is true. There are neither lucky nor unlucky directions. People may agree with this when I talk about directions, but they still think rich is better than poor. Actually, it's not clear which is better. Children who grow up in a rich family may be spoiled and behave coldly toward their parents or fight like enemies over their inheritance.

People often say this or that is reality, as if these are unchangeable truths, but such "reality" is questionable. It's reality only from the standpoint of an ordinary person who mistakes their ideas for the truth.

KOSHO UCHIYAMA:
These days, since many people live in large housing developments, they don't care about directions as people did when they built

their own dwellings. Now we know that east, west, north, and south are relative; they're determined only from a certain position. Similarly, if we think that rich is good, poor is bad, high social status is desirable, or beauty is alluring, we're thinking only from a limited perspective. Such value judgments are only from the viewpoint of an ordinary person.

If we think the delusion of ordinary people is bad and the enlightenment of buddhas is good, we're still viewing from a particular perspective. To stop looking from any point of view is zazen. That's why the Heart Sutra says, "neither arising nor perishing, neither defiled nor pure, neither increasing nor decreasing."

SHOHAKU OKUMURA:

The poem Sawaki Roshi quotes is from the Kokkyoshu of Japanese Rinzai Zen Master Muso Soseki (1275–1351).

In ancient Japanese culture, it was important to know the auspicious or unlucky directions for almost all activities, from major undertakings such as constructing the capital city to minor questions such as where to build a bathroom in a house. People relied on fortunetellers not only for buildings but also for daily activities: for instance, which direction to avoid going on certain days.

These fortunetellers were experts in a kind of divination based on parts of Daoist theory such as yin and yang and feng shui. Such ideas were introduced from China to Japan about fifteen hundred years ago, together with Confucianism, Buddhism, and other aspects of Chinese culture that have since developed in unique ways in Japan. From a modern, scientific way of thinking, these are merely superstitions. And yet feng shui is still quite popular not only in China and Japan but also in the West.

From the Buddhist perspective, as Sawaki Roshi and Uchiyama Roshi say, such ideas about good/bad fortune, positive/negative energy, etc., are not valid as ultimate truth. But some Japanese Buddhists have used them as skillful means, while others respect them as social customs. Here Sawaki Roshi and Uchiyama Roshi explain that practices for pursuing good fortune in the worldly sense are logical only within a limited framework.

In Japan the beautiful goddess of fortune, Kichijoten, and the ugly goddess of misfortune, Kokuanten, are sisters and always appear together. Fortune and misfortune cannot exist independently because they're defined by contrast with each other; they're both relative. When we pursue fortune and succeed, we might be happy, but fortune easily changes to misfortune, and then we suffer. Zazen allows us to transcend this dualistic framework. Beyond fortune and misfortune is nirvana—Sawaki Roshi's "true and final refuge" within this very life.

32.

Zazen Rather Than Money

KODO SAWAKI:
Lately some priests manage inns at their temples. Human beings are wondrous. Some of them don't think about anything besides eating and earning money.

KOSHO UCHIYAMA:
When we venerate an image of the Buddha as the Awakened One, it becomes the Buddha for us. If temple priests fight over the statue or sell it to make money, it becomes only an object of greed.

In today's world, we put absolute value on money. When we think of the value of things, we always calculate in monetary terms as if that's the only valid way. The temple where I live now doesn't have any family members or income. For more than ten years, I've made my living by begging in the city of Kyoto. Occasionally, with misguided kindness, people suggest that since Antaiji sits on a large amount of land, I ought to rent out parking spaces or apartments, or rent the temple for events to generate income.

My reaction to such suggestions is that I don't know what I would do with the money. Antaiji is a Zen temple. If the roof leaks and I can't fix it, I should continue to do zazen in a spot where the water doesn't drip. If the building goes to ruin through lack of repair, but I continue to do zazen, the temple buildings will "become Buddha"—will die peacefully. As long as I can repair the temple, I will. But if I can't, I'll just continue to do zazen.

Sawaki Roshi agreed with my attitude on this point and said, "In my time and in your time, Antaiji is *antai*, is at peace." My deepest wish is that people will continue zazen practice there and maintain Antaiji as it is—a poor temple—not only while I'm abbot, but forever.

How delightful it would be to find some small corner of this world where money is not the absolute value. But when I go begging, people in Kyoto give me small donations and keep me from starving. I'm really grateful for that.

SHOHAKU OKUMURA:
Uchiyama Roshi's opinion about Zen temples came from *Shobogenzo Zuimonki*, in which Dogen Zenji discusses Zen Master Fanghui, who said:

> Even though the building is broken down, it is certainly a better place for practicing zazen than on the ground or under a tree. If one section is broken and leaks, we should move where there are no leaks to practice zazen. If monks could attain enlightenment by building a hall, we should construct one of gold and jewels. Enlightenment does not depend on whether the building is good or bad; it depends only upon our diligence in zazen.

In an essay on his experiences with begging, Uchiyama Roshi wrote about an old craftsman he met on a streetcar. This was during the cherry blossom season, in the spring. People were having parties under the cherry trees in famous spots in Kyoto. The streetcar was quite crowded. Uchiyama Roshi was hanging on to a strap and reading. The old man called to him and invited him to sit. He was drunk after partying. He tried to talk with the monk about this and that, but Roshi kept reading.

The old man became silent for a while, and then said with a sincere voice, "Please practice diligently. While people are enjoying the beautiful cherry blossoms, you're practicing begging. I'm a tinsmith. When kids hear the voices of begging monks, they come into my shop asking for coins. I usually give them two or three yen. The monks receive this small donation, lowering their heads in a very respectful way. You're not such low-class people that you need to accept two or three yen politely. However, please practice diligently. In Kyoto all the great Zen masters such as Ikkyu-san have been practicing begging for many centuries. We laypeople have been offering small donations to the monks, thinking that if we continue supporting monks, great masters like Ikkyu-san will appear again." Uchiyama Roshi bowed to the old man.

Where Buddhist monks support their practice with begging, there have always been people like the old tinsmith who gave to the monks. That was the cultural background in which Sawaki Roshi and Uchiyama Roshi could focus on zazen practice without thinking of money.

But these days even in Japan monks cannot support their practice by begging, so we need to find another way. Many American Zen centers do fundraising to support themselves, or they charge fees for certain kinds of practice. But we need to be careful not to lose the spirit either of practice or donation. Both receivers and givers should try to preserve the attitudes of Uchiyama Roshi and the tinsmith. In the mealtime chant at monasteries, we express our intention to realize the emptiness, the freedom from clinging, of giver, receiver, and gift. Both giver and receiver need to be free of desire and expectation of reward.

33

Feeling Like a King

KODO SAWAKI:
Stop wearing a tearful face! Out of timidity, you think you're worthless and others are superior; you weep and worry about trivia. And if after a while things go well, you become elated.

KOSHO UCHIYAMA:
We never go hungry, even though we don't produce a single grain of rice. We live in houses sheltered from weather, although we can't cut down a tree and saw it into boards. We wear fine clothes though we don't know how to spin cotton into thread. We get light simply by flipping a switch and water by turning a faucet. If we compared our present lifestyle to that of a king in ancient Egypt, we'd see that we live as if we had dozens of slaves.

We can feel how luxurious our lives are when we imagine that we own many slaves who grow grains and vegetables for us to eat, build our houses, weave fabric for our clothes, bring light when it gets dark, carry water for us to drink, and so on. When you use an electric fan, imagine that a handsome attendant cools you. When watching TV, pretend all the entertainers in the country have gathered to display their talents to amuse you, the king. It's fun to lord it over them and say, "Your performance is boring. Who can entertain me better?" and change the channel.

We should stop comparing ourselves with others and feeling inferior all the time. Instead, at least once in a while, we should reflect on ourselves and consider whether we deserve to live so comfortably. How have we come to live in such favorable circumstances? I think this is because we're able to use, free of charge, all the knowledge, skill, and wealth accumulated by human beings since men and women first appeared in this world. I hope we don't forget to have gratitude toward people of the past and devote ourselves to making something meaningful for people in the future.

SHOHAKU OKUMURA:
In the Sutra of the Buddha's Last Teaching, or Yuikyogyo, right before Shakyamuni Buddha passed away, he taught about eight aspects of great beings' awakening; these form the basis for *Shobogenzo Hachidainingaku*. The first two are "having little desire" and "knowing satisfaction."

About having little desire, the Buddha said:

> Monks, you should know that people who have great desires avariciously seek after fame and profit; therefore they have much suffering and anguish. Those who have little desire, because they have nothing to pursue, are free from such troubles. . . . The minds of those who practice having little desire are peaceful, without any worries or fears. They always see themselves as affluent, whatever they have, and never have a sense of insufficiency. Those who have little desire abide in nirvana.

And about knowing satisfaction, he said:

> Monks, if you want to be free of suffering and anguish, you should contemplate knowing how much is enough. The dharma of knowing satisfaction is the place of richness, joy, peace, and calm. Those who know satisfaction, even when they lie on the ground, still consider it comfortable and joyful. Those who don't know satisfaction are discontented even when they are in a heavenly palace. Those who don't know satisfaction are poor even if they have great wealth. Those who know satisfaction are rich even if they are poor.

Sawaki Roshi and Uchiyama Roshi echo Shakyamuni Buddha's final teaching.

The fourth aspect of great beings' awakening is diligence. We need to practice and work diligently with little desire, knowing satisfaction. But when we work hard, our driving force is usually dissatisfaction with current conditions and desire for future reward. Without dissatisfaction and desire, what can be our motivation to work diligently?

Uchiyama Roshi says this energy should flow from our appreciation and gratitude for our predecessors' efforts, and our vow to contribute to future generations. We can exist only within the network of interdependent origination. We need to be grateful for the support of all things past and present, and work diligently as our own offering to this web.

34.

My Opinion

KODO SAWAKI:

Everyone reads the newspaper in a different order. One person reads the stock page first, another turns first to sports or a serialized novel or political columns. We're all different because we see things through our individual discriminating consciousnesses.

Grasping things with our thoughts, we each behave differently. When we stop perceiving with our illusory discriminating consciousnesses, we can experience the world that we share. True reality isn't something we see from our individual perspective. Therefore human beings make mistakes despite careful thinking.

KOSHO UCHIYAMA:

From the street I heard, "We are representatives of such-and-such a party. Let's stand against . . . ." This was over a loudspeaker from a political propaganda car, but I couldn't hear clearly what they objected to. I could only hear them saying, "Let's stand against . . . ! Let's stand against . . . !"

A stone is silently and simply a stone. No stone says whether it's valuable or not. And yet these days, there's a boom in garden stones. Rocks suitable for traditional Japanese gardens seem ridiculously expensive.

Similarly, the true reality of all things exists silently, just as it is, before any evaluation. But when things are viewed through human eyes, we apply different systems, appraising in various ways, and take action accordingly. Inevitably, at the same time, some voices are raised saying, "Let's stand against . . . !"

If these remain mere voices, they don't matter much. But if the voices give rise to fights or even war, which nowadays poses the threat of destroying the world, this is a big problem. Human beings make mistakes despite careful thinking.

Because we have eyes and brains, we can't stop seeing and thinking. However, I hope we understand that the world we see and the things we think are merely stories generated in our heads. We must be careful not to cause serious problems by being turned around by our thoughts. Zazen is a posture that enables us to see through the illusions of our thinking selves.

KODO SAWAKI:
People often say, "In my opinion . . . ." Your opinion is no good—so keep your mouth shut!

SHOHAKU OKUMURA:
In chapter 30, Sawaki Roshi and Uchiyama Roshi talked about people who chase external things and lose sight of themselves. In this chapter they discuss how one's own opinion is not valid. On the surface, these two are contradictory. How can we seek ourselves without having our own opinion?

When the Buddha, Sawaki Roshi, and Uchiyama Roshi talk about "self" they don't mean the image of ourselves created within the framework of separation between *I* as subject and others as objects. In Harischandra Kaviratna's translation of the Dhammapada, the Buddha says, "The self is the master of the self. Who else can that master be? With the self fully subdued, one obtains the sublime refuge, which is very difficult to achieve." Self is master of the self, but the self still needs to be subdued. In the Japanese translation of this verse, "subdued" is more like "harmonized" or "well tuned."

In Genjokoan, Dogen said, "To study the Buddha way is to study the self. To study the self is to forget the self." To study the self, we need to forget the self. In these sayings, self is not a fixed, permanent entity separate from other beings. Self is our body and mind, that is, a collection of the five aggregates: form, sensation, perception, formation, and consciousness. These aggregates are always changing, but somehow we create a fixed self-image based on our past experiences and relations with others. We grasp this image as *I*.

This *I* is an illusion, yet we measure everything based on the tunnel vision of this fictitious self. When we see fiction as fiction, illusion as illusion, they can be useful. Although no map is reality itself, when we know how a map was made, what its distortions are, and how to use it, the map can be a useful tool for understanding reality. However, if we don't see a model's limitations, we build our entire lives on a delusion.

35

Science and Human Beings

KODO SAWAKI:

Science progresses rapidly because researchers base their work on information accumulated by other scientists and then develop their own findings. Human beings cannot cultivate our spirituality the same way, because we can't receive the results of other people's practice and base our own practice on them. Each of us has to start from the beginning. We can't start from the point our teachers reached. This is why human beings with technology are like children playing with lethal weapons. It's very dangerous.

KOSHO UCHIYAMA:

Some people think that in the future, scientific advancement will solve every problem and make everyone wealthy and happy. When I hear someone speaking this way, I think the person is really simpleminded. It's like riding a train thinking happily about the air-conditioned, comfortable first-class coach, while standing in the aisle of a crowded second-class car, covered with sweat on a summer's night.

As science and technology continue to advance, some of the serious problems of the present will be solved. When I was young, my wife died of tuberculosis. If the medicines we have now had been available then, I wouldn't have lost her. I sincerely appreciate scientific progress.

But it's nonsense to think all our problems can be solved through scientific advancement. Science is an endeavor of mankind, and mankind is an abstract concept. Mankind existed ten thousand years ago and will exist ten thousand years from now. On the contrary, each of us has a transitory life of only about seventy or eighty years. In the years given us, it's a real problem that we don't know how to manage our lives.

It's not bad to dream about the future of science, but it's more important to consider the big picture of our short lives and find a place where we can be stable.

SHOHAKU OKUMURA:
Until the 1960s, when Uchiyama Roshi wrote this article, many people thought the world was improving because of the development of science and technology. But since then we have come to understand that science, technology, and the economy based on them are also the main causes of environmental destruction. This is really "an inconvenient truth." Our efforts to make our lives easier and wealthier destroy parts of the network of interdependent origination. Injuring this living network is hurting ourselves in the long run. About fifty years have passed since we recognized this problem, and yet our behavior doesn't seem to be changing much.

Among human beings it seems there are two groups. Some people can take advantage of science and technology to create systems through which they can make money; these are the passengers in the first-class cabin. Another group is in the second-class coach without air-conditioning. It's said that 99 percent of human beings are in the second group, and 1 percent own 99 percent of the wealth on earth.

More than half of humanity is starving or undernourished, and yet people in developed countries suffer from overeating. This isn't a healthy condition for anyone. We need to work on transforming our situation. A contribution we can make from Buddhist tradition is the teaching of living with little desire and knowing satisfaction, and working diligently not merely to satisfy our wants but to maintain the health of the entire network of interdependent origination.

36

Loss

KODO SAWAKI:

To study Buddhism is to study loss. Shakyamuni Buddha is a good example. He left his father's palace, his beautiful wife, his lovely child, and gave up his splendid clothes to become a beggar. He practiced begging with bare feet and a shabby robe for the rest of his life. All the buddhas and ancestors suffer loss intentionally.

It's a big mistake if we become Buddhist monks hoping to be successful in the world. No matter what, we monks are beggars from head to toe.

KOSHO UCHIYAMA:

For us ordinary human beings, the easiest thing to understand is whether we gain or lose. Our fundamental premise is that gaining is better than losing. From such a viewpoint, Shakyamuni Buddha was a very strange person. He walked the path of loss without thinking of gain. Why did he begin on such a path? All conditioned things are impermanent; therefore the criteria of loss and gain are constantly changing. Shakyamuni Buddha saw this limitation of the path of gain and loss and renounced it. He chose a path beyond gain and loss. He intentionally walked the path of loss to show us the way beyond gaining and losing.

We ordinary people always dream of gain without loss. The path beyond loss and gain is the life of the stable self that exists before separation between subject and object; it is beyond the duality of lucky and unlucky, rich and poor, superior and inferior. If we're poor, it's fine to be poor. Right there, we can find a dignified stability. If we're sick, there too we can find a dignified stability. When we live with this attitude, there's absolute stability in the Dharma no matter what conditions we experience.

KODO SAWAKI:

All sentient beings are busy making mistakes. They think their unhappy affairs are happy and their happy affairs are unhappy, and are always kicking and screaming. When you give a piece of candy to a crying child, the kid grins with eyes full of tears. The happiness that sentient beings speak of is no better than this.

SHOHAKU OKUMURA:

Sawaki Roshi's description of monks as beggars means those who live not by pursuing personal possessions but rather by working for the Dharma and entrusting their lives to all beings in the universe. This is the same as being "homeless," as Sawaki Roshi and Uchiyama Roshi discussed in chapter 1.

In *Shobogenzo Zuimonki*, Koun Ejo, Dharma successor of Dogen Zenji, asked his teacher, "As an activity of Zen practitioners, mending or patching old or tattered clothing instead of throwing it away seems to be clinging to things. Yet abandoning old clothing and wearing new robes shows we're seeking after new things. Both of these are wrong. Ultimately, what should we do?"

Dogen answered, "If we're free from holding on to what we have, yet do not seek after what we don't have, either way is all right. Still, it would be better to mend torn clothing, in order to keep it for as long as possible and not pursue acquiring new clothing."

This is one of my favorite conversations between Dogen and Ejo in *Shobogenzo Zuimonki*. Dogen was born into one of the most prestigious noble families of his time. If he hadn't become a Buddhist monk, he could have been a high government official. Even after he became a monk, if he had stayed within the Tendai school, he would have been a high-ranking priest and teacher to the emperor or aristocracy. He inherited some family property but spent all his wealth to fund travel to China.

According to his biography, Ejo was from the Fujiwara family, the most powerful in the emperor's court. After he became a well-known scholar monk at Mount Hiei, he visited his mother. She said she allowed him to become a monk not because she wanted him to rise to a high position. She advised him not to study or practice merely for fame and profit. She hoped he would wear a simple black robe, hang a bamboo hat on his back, and walk on his own feet instead of riding in a fancy carriage.

Dogen and Ejo both left home and became Buddhist monks at Enryakuji monastery on Mount Hiei. And both eventually left the Tendai order to seek the genuine practice of the buddha way. Because they left home and the Buddhist establishment, they were poor.

One day, after Ejo had begun practicing with Dogen at the newly established Koshoji monastery, these two masters, eminent in the history of Buddhism, seriously discussed whether to mend their shabby robes or try to get new ones. To me, this is a moving conversation. Both were brilliant people from noble families. They could have taken advantage of their status and become powerful leaders. Instead, because of their aspirations and vows, they lived in poverty and considered how best to practice with their circumstances, with their old robes.

These teachers chose a life based not on conventional ideas of gain and loss, success and failure, happiness and sadness, but on simply working as much as possible for the sake of the Dharma and receiving whatever was offered by life.

37.

Halfway Zazen

KODO SAWAKI:
There is a book titled *Zen and the Cultivation of Hara*. Such hara is nothing but numbness and apathy.

SHOHAKU OKUMURA:
The *hara* is about three inches below the navel. In traditional Chinese medicine, this part of the body is considered the center of one's being, or the field for cultivating *ki* (in Chinese: *qi*). For example, in aikido it's important to move from the hara. In Japanese martial arts, cultivating the strength of the hara is essential. Since many of these arts are combined with Zen training, zazen is often considered a method of strengthening the hara. But the idea of training the hara originated in martial arts rather than Buddhist teachings.

When Sawaki Roshi was a soldier during the Russo-Japanese War, he felt no fear on the battlefield, and everyone praised his courage. He even received the highest military honor. Sometime after he returned from the war and started to study Buddhism, he was startled by an explosion at a nearby fireworks factory. He then realized his bravery in battle was actually a kind of stupor, and fear was more natural.

At least in Japan, a common misunderstanding is that zazen is training for becoming fearless. But Sawaki Roshi says this kind of fearlessness is nothing but obliviousness and moral apathy.

KODO SAWAKI:
A Zen *tenma*, or heavenly demon, is an ordinary person practicing to gain satori, to become great.

Buddhadharma is not something for making an ordinary person great.

People say you can cultivate the hara by doing zazen. To know that we don't need such hara is the real hara, the true stability.

KOSHO UCHIYAMA:
Some people take for granted that the goal of Zen practice is to achieve satori and become courageous. Others believe that Zen is an evil practice. But the zazen transmitted by Shakyamuni Buddha, Bodhidharma, Dogen Zenji, and Sawaki Roshi is nothing other than a true religion that teaches us to take final refuge in this life.

True zazen is not something that satisfies an ordinary human being's half-baked desires, such as the desire to make money or succeed in the world—even to find a cure for a disease. Such desires are half-baked because all these achievements must be cast aside when we die. Satisfying these desires cannot be a stable way of living as long as we can die at any moment. The other side of our life is death.

For the same reason, the zazen that gives us satori and the courage to frighten off the bill collector with a yell is also half-baked. Any teaching that professes to make an ordinary person great is a heavenly demon.

The zazen Sawaki Roshi taught is not a practice by which an ordinary person satisfies desires or becomes great. From the standpoint of ordinary human beings, the zazen he taught is good for nothing; it's simply the practice of true religion. He taught zazen as stability in life, which enables us to settle within the Buddhadharma: beyond separation between subject and object, birth and death, enlightenment and delusion. This is the zazen that accords with the reality of neither arising nor ceasing, neither defiled nor pure, neither increasing nor decreasing.

SHOHAKU OKUMURA:
When we have difficulties, we might start to practice zazen to find a way out. Some people seek worldly success with meditation, using it as training in concentration, spontaneity, or bravery. Others aspire to be released from everyday life by some kind of enlightenment experience. Either way, we search because we feel a lack.

When we practice zazen with this attitude, what happens in our minds is the same as when we struggle for fame and profit. As long as we practice zazen with seeking mind, we create samsara within our practice. We're not happy now, but we think if we find something to fill our emptiness, we'll be happy, so we pursue that object. Sometimes we succeed and feel like heavenly beings; other times we're disappointed, like ghosts hungry for enlightenment, or hell-dwellers. When we feel like heavenly beings, with confidence in attaining enlightenment, we become arrogant. This is the Zen tenma, or heavenly demon, of Sawaki Roshi's saying.

This expression was first coined by Nichiren (1222–82) as part of his criticism of the four influential Buddhist schools of his time: Shingon, Zen, Pure Land, and Ritsu, or Vinaya. Nichiren maintained that Zen was a heavenly demon, meaning an evil practice. Here Sawaki Roshi uses this expression to mean that if we practice zazen to transform this ordinary, deluded human being into an enlightened one, such zazen is really being done by the demon Mara. The heavenly demon is not something outside ourselves that controls us; this demon is us when we cling to this self as *I*.

Receiving gifts or blessings from our practice is no problem as long as they aren't our motivation; if they are, then we're only doing "halfway zazen."

38

Seeing According to Karmic Consciousness

KODO SAWAKI:

There's only one moon, but sometimes it looks happy, sometimes sad. Sometimes we drink sake while enjoying the moonlight. Each moon that we human beings see depends on the condition of our karmic consciousness; it's not the real moon.

KOSHO UCHIYAMA:

That the moon corresponds to the condition of one's karmic consciousness means that the way we see the moon is conditioned by the experiences we've had since birth.

For example, these days, there must be scientists and engineers who look at the moon and think, "How can we get a rocket carrying a man to make a soft landing on that heavenly body?" There might be geologists who look at the moon thinking, "What are its geological features?" The moon may look radiant to a person at the peak of prosperity and melancholy to someone who has hit bottom. For a drinker, the moon is nothing other than an appetizer with sake.

In Japanese we have expressions such as *go no fukai ningen*, a person with deep karma, and *go tsukubari*, a person whose karma is very strong. These expressions refer to those with extreme conditioned viewpoints, partly as a result of intense life experiences.

Buddhism is often misunderstood as a teaching of resignation that makes us think, "I can't help it . . . it's my karma." Such a teaching cannot be true Buddhism. Instead, Buddhism teaches us to soften our rigid karmic standpoint, deconstruct the illusory views of the karmic self, and see life as it is.

KODO SAWAKI:

Go kan, or seeing according to one's karma, is one's good or bad past actions extending into the present. For example, a widow who has lived her whole life obsessed with sex might be jealous of young couples.

Ordinary human beings are pulled by their karma and view the world only according to their karmic conditions. Such people continue undesirable yet unseverable relations with each other, one lifetime after another. This is called "perpetual wandering within samsara."

If we take off the colored glasses of karmic consciousness, then as Shakyamuni said when he attained enlightenment, we will see that "the great earth and all sentient beings simultaneously attain the way; mountains and rivers, grasses and trees, all things without exception become buddha."

SHOHAKU OKUMURA:

When he was young, Sawaki Roshi studied the "Consciousness Only" teaching of Yogacara, one of the two Mahayana schools, at Horyuji temple in Nara. According to Yogacara, our consciousness has eight layers. The first five are caused by contact between the sense organs and their objects: eye, ear, nose, tongue, and body consciousnesses. The sixth consciousness is caused by contact between our minds and the objects of mind, such as numbers and ideas.

Yogacara masters also identified two layers below our thinking minds. The seventh layer is called *manas*, often translated into English as "ego consciousness," and the eighth is *alaya*, or "storehouse," consciousness. In Yogacara understanding, all our past experiences are stored as seeds within this deepest layer. The manas consciousness grasps this collection of stored seeds as *I* and controls our first six consciousnesses.

When we encounter an object, the seeds in the storehouse are activated and our perception is influenced by them, not simply by the object as it is. Depending which seeds are stored in the deepest layer of our consciousness, people's interpretations of and reactions to the same objects are different. But commonly we assume that what we see is how the object actually exists.

In Yogacara teaching, through our practice of understanding everything as merely perception, we free ourselves from karmic consciousness and begin to view things as they are. Then the eight layers of consciousness begin to function as four kinds of wisdom: the storehouse consciousness is transformed into the Great Perfect Mirror wisdom that reflects things as they are, the ego consciousness begins to work as the wisdom that sees the equality of all things, the sixth consciousness lets us see objects with the wisdom that skillfully observes, and the first five consciousnesses enable us to act with wisdom. In Yogacara, consciousness is analyzed from shallow to deep layers, whereas wisdom is explained from deep to shallow, reflecting the idea that lasting change must begin at the deepest level of our consciousness. Otherwise, if a change in perception occurs merely at the level of our thinking mind, it's likely to be momentary and confined to certain objects.

In Japan, Yogacara traditionally has been considered the basis of Buddhist theory, similar to Abhidharma. It's considered more fundamental than the teachings of popular Mahayana schools such as Kegon, Tendai, and Shingon, which are valued as the pinnacle of Mahayana philosophy. In Sawaki Roshi's Zen teachings, we see the influence of Yogacara.

39.

Aborting the Self

KODO SAWAKI:
Zazen is like re-entering our mother's womb. Therefore, it is not a means to an end.

KOSHO UCHIYAMA:
A boy fell into bad company and became a juvenile delinquent. He frequently extorted money from his mother and idled his time away.

One day he happened to meet his mother on the street and demanded money. The mother couldn't stand it any longer and scolded him, "Why do you assume I have money for you? You're old enough to be independent, but you have no intention of finding a job. Why do you always give me trouble?"

The son replied, "Although I didn't ask you to give birth to me, you always find fault with me. Why did you have me?" For most parents, this is the most difficult question to answer. When I was around twenty, and my parents criticized me for this or that, I would say, "Why did you have me?" Then they immediately fell silent.

But from this story, I see the mothers of the post-war generation are stronger and smarter. She retorted, "Oh, too bad. You've grown too big for me to put you back in my womb. Become small again and go back. If you can do that, I'll gladly have an abortion."

Someone told me this story the other day. Whenever I heard an interesting story like this, I used to tell it to Sawaki Roshi while serving him tea. He's not alive anymore, and I feel lonely. But I think if he had heard this story, he would have said, "Zazen is the posture in which the self is aborted before being born."

SHOHAKU OKUMURA:

In this book, Sawaki Roshi and Uchiyama Roshi express the meaning of zazen in various ways:

> Chapter 6: "Zazen is the self selfing the self."
> Chapter 12: "Our practice of zazen is looking at the world afresh after being in hibernation."
> Chapter 21: "To practice zazen is to stop being an ordinary human being."
> Chapter 26: "Zazen is seeing this world from the casket, without *me*."
> Chapter 31: "To stop looking from any point of view is zazen."
> Chapter 37: "True zazen is not something that satisfies an ordinary human being's half-baked desires."
> Chapter 37: "From the standpoint of ordinary human beings, the zazen he taught is good for nothing; it's simply the practice of true religion."

And in this chapter, Sawaki Roshi says: "Zazen is like re-entering our mother's womb. Therefore, it is not a means to an end." A baby is simply being itself peacefully, without desire to achieve anything. The baby and womb are one and yet not the same, like a person sitting zazen in the world.

This expression most likely came from the Buddhist idea of *tathagata-garbha*, which means "embryo buddha." The image has two sides: buddha-nature is an embryo living within us, and also we are the baby buddha within the womb of the tathagatha, the awakened one.

The expression "aborted before being born" is equivalent to Sawaki Roshi's explanation of zazen as looking at the world from a coffin; both mean that zazen isn't about fulfilling our human desires. Between birth and death we need to consider our responsibilities, but in zazen each of us is like an embryo or a dead person. The expression "before being born" also echoes the koan question "What was your original face before your parents were born?"

Sawaki Roshi expresses zazen as the practice of Buddhadharma, beyond our personal desires for various kinds of profit. In Buddhism there are two aspects of the teaching: worldly and beyond worldly. Roughly speaking, these parallel the distinction between conventional and ultimate truth. Zazen is beyond-worldly practice that has nothing to do with our expectation of reward.

The conversation between Bodhidharma and Emperor Wu in *The Blue Cliff Record* is a good example. Emperor Wu asked, "I have built temples and allowed many monks to be ordained; what merit is there in this?" Bodhidharma answered, "No merit." The Emperor asked, "What is the ultimate meaning of the sacred truth?" Bodhidharma replied, "Empty, nothing sacred."

Emperor Wu is speaking from worldly Dharma, and Bodhidharma is responding from beyond-worldly Dharma. When Dogen Zenji said we should practice without gaining mind, he was also speaking from beyond-worldly Dharma.

Zazen should not be defiled by our desires—even the desire for enlightenment or becoming a buddha.

40

What's the Point of Working to Get Rich?

KODO SAWAKI:
People believe that living in the lap of luxury is something great. It's strange to me that people are respected because they have money.

KOSHO UCHIYAMA:
I once overheard a conversation between two housewives. One's husband was an average salaried worker who probably earned fifty or sixty thousand yen a month. The second wife said proudly, "In my family, we need at least two hundred thousand yen a month. We recently bought a new car for our child." The first woman listened to this with awe and envy.

However, if the second woman were unexpectedly invited to a social gathering of very rich, high-society women, she would probably feel timidity and fear. This world is a strange place. In truth, a fifty- or sixty-thousand-yen income is not small, nor is a two-hundred-thousand-yen income great. However it seems simple-minded people believe a person's income is their value.

If a woman has such a belief, and her husband, tired of earning their living with his hard and boring work, says that when he reaches retirement age, he'd like to stop working and practice zazen, I'm sure his wife will say, "What about our livelihood? You don't have spare time to do zazen!" She'll grab him by his collar, pull him up, and apply the whip. He'll have to struggle to his feet with his tired body and gaspingly continue to walk in the world of loss and gain with the "assistance" of his wife. This would be so pitiful that a soft-hearted person like me would not be able to look him in the face.

KODO SAWAKI:

If we don't pay attention, human beings get caught up in the frenzy of earning a living.

People always say they're busy. For what are they busy? Only to earn their bread. Chickens also look busy constantly eating. But they eat only to be eaten.

SHOHAKU OKUMURA:

When I was a child, people said that in the future, because of the development of technology, we'd be released from hard work and have more time to enjoy our lives. In a sense, this has proven true. In most developed countries today, many people work only five days a week and can take week-long or even month-long vacations. However, it seems leisure makes our lives even busier and more tiring. We have to form long lines at train stations or airports to get out of cities. We have to drive busy highways during endless traffic jams. Sometimes, a hundred miles of the highway is like a parking lot. When we return home from vacation, we're more tired than after our busy workdays.

Sawaki Roshi told a funny story. There was a village where people were so lazy that they were in extreme poverty. A person came to the village and tried to teach them that they should work hard for a better life. The villagers asked, "What's the point of working hard?" The person answered, "So you can make money and become rich." The villagers asked, "What's the point of being rich?" The person replied, "If you have a lot of money, you won't need to work." The villagers said, "But that's what we do now."

41

Pitiful Heavenly Beings

KODO SAWAKI:
Most people don't live by their own strength. They merely feed off the power of organizations. Those who make a living by their titles or status are wimps.

KOSHO UCHIYAMA:
The concept of the heavenly being in Buddhism is very interesting when we carefully examine it. Heavenly beings dwell in the clouds and enjoy luxurious lives in paradise—but they don't have any real power.

If this is true, then modern people are heavenly beings dwelling in the clouds known as contemporary civilization. Without exception we moderns would starve to death if we were thrown out into nature. And yet because we're riding on the clouds of social organizations, we're able to live comfortably. Despite this, we're always complaining.

If the president of a company that has constructed a huge building thinks that he built the building, he's making a great mistake. He's just accidentally at the top of an organization that has the power to accumulate money to construct such a building. He himself could not make—or carry!—a single piece of reinforcing iron rod. Yet modern people go crazy scrambling for illusory power in the clouds of the social system.

Although such organizations look stable and solid, they're really as ephemeral and unreliable as clouds. Hitler once lived in the monstrous clouds of fascism, but in the end he was alone. When the clouds of organization dissipate, heavenly beings are compelled to realize how powerless they are, and at this moment they fall to earth. A song says, "Heavenly beings grieve over the five signs of decay." How pitiful when their celestial robes get soiled and tattered. The higher they've climbed in heaven, the more they suffer when they fall.

KODO SAWAKI:
It's a mistake to climb to a higher place, from which you'll just have to fall, sooner or later. "No place to fall" is the life of a home-leaver.

SHOHAKU OKUMURA:
In the traditional Buddhism described in the *Abhidharmakosa*, heaven is not a single, permanent place like in Christianity. Heaven has many layers, and beings can't live there forever. Beings abiding in the twenty-eight realms of heaven enjoy long lives filled with pleasure and access to various divine powers. And yet they still exist within samsara, the burning house. Their life span is much longer than that of human beings, but still their lives end.

When they age and are about to leave heaven for lower realms, it's said in the Mahayana Parinirvana Sutra that they show five signs of decline: their robes become dirty, the flower decorations on their heads fade, their bodies smell, they sweat under their arms, and they do not enjoy their seats in heaven. Apparently the suffering they experience when they tumble from heaven is sixteen times the misery of hell dwellers.

Uchiyama Roshi says that modern people in developed countries who enjoy convenient lives without personal effort are like these heavenly beings. People at the top especially enjoy their lives. However, everything is impermanent. When they lose status, they experience much suffering, just like the heavenly beings of ancient Buddhist cosmology.

Heaven is a manmade idea of what's "better." When we feel more successful than others, we're in heaven. When we feel others are more successful, we're in hell. To leave this way of life based on comparison is to free ourselves from samsara. Living on the ground of the true reality of life is finding nirvana within this world.

42

Only When We Practice

KODO SAWAKI:

Religion is not for changing the external world. It is for transforming our eyes and ears, our habitual ways of perceiving and thinking.

KOSHO UCHIYAMA:

There was a man who behaved strangely when he drank sake. Whenever he was drunk, he wanted to talk about zazen. When this person visited Antaiji for the first time and said he wanted to talk with Sawaki Roshi, I didn't know of his habit, so I allowed the meeting. What the man said was totally incoherent; he was simply babbling. Since I didn't want Sawaki Roshi to get tired, I convinced the visitor to leave, after great effort.

When he came next and asked to meet with Sawaki Roshi, I remembered what had happened the last time and noticed from his breath that he was drunk. I didn't let him meet with Sawaki Roshi but received him myself. Again, he started to say this and that about zazen, so I said, "If you want to talk about zazen, come back when you're sober. When you sit zazen, the world of zazen opens itself without your saying anything. When you're drunk, whatever you say is simply taking place within the world of drinking. Everything you're saying now is just a drinking game."

KODO SAWAKI:

Ishikawa Goemon, the famous thief whose family name means "stone river," said in a verse, "Even if the sands of the beach or the stone river might be exhausted, in this world the seeds of the thief will never be eliminated." This means that thief-nature permeates the entire universe. And yet we don't actually become thieves unless we imitate Goemon and steal things. Buddha-nature also permeates the entire universe; however you will never become a buddha unless you imitate the Buddha and practice. We are buddhas only when we practice Buddha's practice.

Religion isn't an idea. It's something we practice.

Our practice of religion must be real. It isn't evidence of our virtue.

SHOHAKU OKUMURA:

In his first teaching, Shakyamuni said he had found the middle way. This middle way was the Eightfold Noble Path: right view, right thinking, right speech, right action, right livelihood, right effort, right mindfulness, and right meditation. He taught this path as the last of the Four Noble Truths—the path to the cessation of suffering.

On the day Buddha entered nirvana, the wandering ascetic Subbadha asked, "There are various religious teachers. They teach different teachings to their students. Have they all gained knowledge through their own wisdom, or have none of them any knowledge, or do some have knowledge and others do not?"

The Buddha told Subbhada not to get caught in metaphysical speculation, but to live within the truth. He said, "Never mind whether they have all gained knowledge through their own wisdom or not. Where the Eightfold Noble Path is not found, there are no enlightened practitioners. Where the Eightfold Noble Path is found, there are enlightened practitioners. If monks were to live correctly, there would be no lack of enlightened people."

Shakyamuni taught how to live the middle way, free of extremes of self-indulgence and self-mortification. Then, to explain the middle way, philosophical systems were established in various lineages of Buddhism. Many people simply studied these philosophies without actually living the Eightfold Noble Path. Such people are like bank tellers who count other people's money.

Reading about zazen is the same—like counting other people's money or studying recipes without cooking and tasting. Even if a medicine has hundreds of benefits, reading about them won't cure us.

43

Zazen Is the Stability of One's Whole Life

KODO SAWAKI:
We don't practice to *attain* enlightenment. We practice *dragged around* by enlightenment.

KOSHO UCHIYAMA:
Having a love affair is ecstasy, but marriage is everyday life. In life, there are rainy, windy, and stormy days. It's natural that we cannot always whisper "I'm happy" to each other. We can say the same of zazen. There are two streams of zazen that have been transmitted in Japan. One understands zazen as ecstasy; the other accepts zazen as everyday life.

Buddhist teachings are based on the idea of oneness of subject and object, self and other. A difference occurs depending whether we taste the samadhi of the identity of self and other as an ecstatic psychological condition, or if we just practice it in our daily lives. The former practice is often expressed through art, while the latter is actualized simply within our everyday life based on religion, on the truth and its teaching.

Those who express the samadhi of oneness through various art forms enable others to taste the same kind of ecstasy. I think the Zen introduced by D. T. Suzuki to the world is of this kind.

On the contrary, the zazen that has been transmitted from Dogen Zenji to Sawaki Roshi is nothing other than religion. This is the same as Shinran's *nembutsu*, as chanting the name of Amitabha Buddha. Within our everyday lives, we practice in the midst of delusion, without knowing whether we will fall to hell or be born in the Pure Land.

Our zazen and Shinran's nembutsu are done without thinking of outcomes; we practice without expectations. Religious practice isn't something to show off, nor something we can appreciate by seeing others' performances. It exists within our efforts just to be ourselves. In everyday life, there are rainy, windy, and stormy days, but whatever conditions we may encounter, we just continue to sit as the stability of our entire lives. Sawaki Roshi taught this kind of zazen.

KODO SAWAKI:
We are watched by zazen, scolded by zazen, obstructed by zazen, dragged around by zazen, and spend our lives in tears. This is the happiest life, isn't it?

SHOHAKU OKUMURA:
In his great work *Zen and Japanese Culture*, Daisetsu T. Suzuki wrote about the influence of Zen on many aspects of Japanese culture, including the way of samurai, visual arts such as *sumie* painting and calligraphy, Zen gardens, tea ceremony, and poetry. In this book, Suzuki wrote:

> The greatest productions of art, whether painting, music, sculpture, or poetry, have invariably this quality— something approaching the work of God. The artist, at the moment when his creativeness is at its height, is transformed into an agent of the creator. This supreme moment in the life of an artist, when expressed in Zen terms, is the experience of satori. To experience satori is to become conscious of the Unconscious (*mushin*, no-mind), psychologically speaking. Art has always something of the Unconscious about it. . . . Every art has its mystery, its spiritual rhythm, its *myo* (Ch. *miao*), as the Japanese would call it. As we have seen, this is where Zen becomes most intimately related to all branches of art. The true artist, like a Zen master, is one who knows how to appreciate the *myo* of things.

Uchiyama Roshi emphasizes that the zazen practice transmitted from Dogen Zenji to Sawaki Roshi differs from D. T. Suzuki's Zen.

For example, Dogen Zenji described the oneness of a practitioner and other people and objects, using the example of a cook and his work with colleagues, ingredients, firewood, and water, as well as those who eat the food. In "Tenzokyokun," or "Instructions for the Cook," in *Dogen's Pure Standards for the Zen Community*, he wrote, "All day and all night, things come to mind and the mind attends to them; at one with them all, diligently carry on the Way." Here there's no mysterious satori, or becoming conscious of the Unconscious. There's only sincere, wholehearted practice in ordinary activities.

Uchiyama Roshi observes that Dogen Zenji's zazen has the same characteristics as Shinran's nembutsu. "Practice in the midst of delusions" is Dogen Zenji's saying from Gakudo-yojinshu, or "Points to Watch in Practicing the Way." "Without knowing whether we will fall to hell or be born in the Pure Land" is a paraphrase of Shinran's expression in *Tannisho: Lamenting the Deviations*. Usually Zen is considered a practice powered by the individual, while Shinran's Pure Land Buddhism is salvation by other power. But Uchiyama Roshi says that Dogen Zenji's and Sawaki Roshi's zazen is closer to Shinran's nembutsu than Suzuki's Zen. Shinran teaches that once our faith is established, we are already born in the Pure Land, so his nembutsu is not a prayer for the future but an expression of gratitude for what already exists. According to Uchiyama Roshi, Dogen's zazen is the same.

We cannot expect any ecstasy greater than right here, right now—our everyday lives.

44.

Being Overly Self-Conscious

KODO SAWAKI:
Because grownups have twisted, habitual ways of thinking, we make a big fuss over a single word. Babies, on the other hand, don't care; no matter how hard we try to put a baby to shame, they don't feel shame at all. Only adults can bring disgrace upon themselves or be offended by others, because we have a sense of separation from others and are hypnotized by ourselves. Just walk straightforwardly without getting caught in entanglements.

KOSHO UCHIYAMA:
Although Sawaki Roshi seemed manly, broad-minded, and carefree, he was also careful and behaved prudently. In contrast, although I'm his disciple and act open and undefended, I'm very nervous and anxious. I feel ashamed about almost everything. For example, in the middle of ceremonies, I often become flustered beyond control and so confused that I make big blunders. Afterward I feel so ashamed I wish I could disappear.

However, because I have been very sensitive since childhood, in self-defense I finally had to settle into the stability of "Whatever happens, I am I." After all, there's no end to worrying about how to keep up appearances in this world, and it's impossible to survive as such a fainthearted person.

When I have butterflies in my stomach, that's fine. When I make a big mess of something, what can I do besides accept it? There's nothing else to do. Ultimately, the stability of "Whatever happens, I am I" is zazen as religion. Within this practice more than any other, a person like me can find salvation. I'm very grateful for this. Even if we don't become an expert—always prepared, refined, and elegant like a veteran swordsman, virtuoso Noh actor, or tea master—we're fine, aren't we? What's wrong with toddling and limping along the path of life practicing zazen?

KODO SAWAKI:
To know there's no gap we might fall into from buddhahood is *issaichi*, or all-knowing wisdom. The night train carries you even when you're sleeping.

SHOHAKU OKUMURA:
Sawaki Roshi's phrase "hypnotized by ourselves" means reacting according to our karma, our conditioning, without thinking. When we investigate our daily actions, we find many of them seem almost programmed—we do them without knowing why. If we don't worry so much about evaluations by others, we're more free to walk a straightforward path, and even if we stumble or limp along, that's okay.

In his essay "Dogen Zen as Religion" in the book *Heart of Zen*, Uchiyama Roshi wrote:

> In any case, the absolute prerequisite for a truly religious teaching is that people should not be chosen on the basis of secular values. They should be unconditionally saved and be able to settle in peace. And this is actually possible because religious values belong to a totally different dimension than secular values. I believe that Dogen Zenji used the expressions "universally" and "do not consider whether you are clever or stupid, and do not think of whether you are superior or inferior" to demonstrate that his practice of zazen is nothing other than the universal truth or genuine religion. In the New Testament we find, "He makes His sun to rise on the evil and the good and He pours rain upon the just and the unjust" (Matthew 5:45). A true religion must contain absolute nondifferentiation, no class distinction, universality, and be removed from any

124 | the zen teaching of homeless kodo

discriminatory points of view. Most of all, I want to make absolutely clear that the practice of zazen Dogen Zenji recommended is that of a universal religion.

In this essay, Uchiyama Roshi called D. T. Suzuki's Zen "Adept Zen" and said the goal of Dogen Zenji's zazen is not satori or enlightenment, but peaceful settling of all kinds of people within themselves regardless of their capabilities.

Uchiyama Roshi's expression "toddling or limping along" echoes Zen Master Yaoshan's saying: "Somehow I manage my life in old age, being shaky and tired, with hundreds of mess-ups and thousands of fumblings." Yaoshan, a disciple of Shitou Xiqian in the Soto Zen lineage, coined the expression "think of not-thinking."

Sawaki Roshi fit the stereotype of a Zen master: manly and tough. But there's another reality: the master who's comfortable admitting shortcomings and mistakes.

45

A Holy Man

KODO SAWAKI:
Someone said, "When I listen to Sawaki-san's talks, my faith loses enthusiasm." I speak on purpose to make people's faith fade away; it's simply superstitious faith. Another said, "Although I listen to Sawaki-san's talks, faith doesn't appear." This means my talks don't give birth to superstitious faith.

KOSHO UCHIYAMA:
Once in a while, people abandon dogs or cats on the grounds of our temple. We can't keep them because we have a five-day sesshin each month. We have no choice but to ask someone else to adopt them.

These abandoned animals wag their tails and nestle up to us as if they were trying to charm us into keeping them. I feel really sorry for them. Why don't they try to live on their own instead of looking for a master? Once a dog has an owner and is taken for a walk on a leash, it meets other dogs that could be friends, yet it becomes overbearing and wants to fight. It jumps on people too. On the other hand, if its owner scolds and hits it, it obeys without any resistance at all. I don't understand the psychology of such dogs.

However, it seems many people seek a holy person to worship just as a dog looks for a master. As long as there's demand, supply will appear. These are the gurus who are worshiped. Sadly, despite being only human beings, such gurus try to act larger than life to meet their believers' expectations.

Religion should not exist to satisfy the needs of believers as a master satisfies the needs of his dog. Religion is for people who want to live a life of freedom and integrity based on true reality. In Christianity it's said that a minister who is so great that God becomes veiled in clouds is a bad minister.

KODO SAWAKI:
Some religious leaders work hard to build their image and think they're successful when they become attractive to their believers and are worshiped.

A holy priest says, "I will remain celibate my whole life." There are many disguises for human beings.

SHOHAKU OKUMURA:
Buddhism distinguishes two kinds of faith: one based on understanding, the other on trust in a teacher.

An example of the former is digging a well. When we start to dig, we don't see any water. As we keep digging, we begin to see the soil becoming wet. Then, even though we don't have water yet, we believe that if we continue, we'll reach water sooner or later. This is because of our understanding that wet soil is a sign of water.

In the second kind of faith, even if we don't understand the teaching, we believe it because of our trust in the teacher. The best example of this faith is from Shinran, the founder of Japanese Shin Buddhism. When his believers visited him asking how to attain birth in the Pure Land, he replied, in Taitetsu Unno's translation:

> As for myself, Shinran, I simply receive the words of my dear teacher, Honen, "Just say the nembutsu and be saved by Amida," and entrust myself to the Primal Vow. Besides this, there is nothing else.
>
> I really do not know whether the nembutsu may be the cause of my birth in the Pure Land, or the act that shall condemn me to hell. But I have nothing to regret, even if I should have been deceived by my teacher, and saying the nembutsu, fall into hell. The reason is that if I were capable of realizing Buddhahood by other religious practices and yet fell into hell for saying the nembutsu, I might have dire regrets for having been deceived. But since I am absolutely

incapable of any [other] religious practice, hell is my only home.

As beginners, we need this kind of trust in teachers and faith in the teaching. However, we also must be careful and examine whether we merely worship the teacher or are sincerely searching for the truth, the Dharma, for ourselves. Even among Sawaki Roshi's students, Uchiyama Roshi said, there were people who were attracted by his karmic attributes instead of following his Dharma teaching and practice.

According to the Dhammapada, at Buddha's death, his grieving disciples asked how they could continue their practice without him. His answer could be translated as either "The Dharma and you yourself are your lamp" or "The Dharma and you yourself are your island refuge in the river."

In the Buddhist world, celibacy among priests was considered important. For example, in Sawaki Roshi's time, abbots of Rinzai monasteries were required to be celibate. So some priests used this vow as a kind of cosmetic, to advertise their sincerity and attract followers.

46.

The Despair of the Ordinary Person

KODO SAWAKI:
To lead a religious life is to reflect upon and examine ourselves and our lives.

KOSHO UCHIYAMA:
Sometimes I imagine being sent to prison. I don't know what our society will be like in the future. If it becomes a nation under someone like Hitler, Stalin, or Mao Zedong, I could be imprisoned if the authorities found fault with me.

Someone wrote, "To confine a small number of people in prison is to set the majority at ease with the thought, 'I'm not as bad as they are.'" I'm not sure whether only those in prison are bad. I don't feel it's right to have conceited thoughts like "I'm not as bad as that official who was jailed for corruption."

Furthermore, when I honestly evaluate myself in the ultimate light of religion, I can't help thinking I do so many self-centered things that I should receive a sentence of hell, rather than jail. Would my excuse, "I'm sorry," allow me to avoid hell? No! In the absolute world, no excuse works.

The Kanfugenbosatsugyohokyo, or Sutra of Meditation on the Practice of Samantabhadra Bodhisattva, says, "If you wish to make repentance, sit upright and be mindful of the true reality." Sitting upright in zazen is the posture we arrive at when we reflect honestly on ourselves.

When I apply this to myself, when I judge myself honestly, I always despair. But I resolve to practice zazen, telling myself, "This is only the despair of an ordinary human being." Isn't this desperation the fuel for awakening to the absolute beyond individual views?

KODO SAWAKI:
Life is full of contradictions. We criticize someone, saying, "Look! He did such a terrible thing!" And yet, sometimes that thing is exactly what we want to do.

The calmer we become, the more clearly we see how terrible we are.

Shikantaza, just sitting, is the highest point that ordinary human beings can reach with our bodies.

SHOHAKU OKUMURA:
There are three types of standards for judging human beings: civic laws, social morality, and religious guidelines. Laws judge only our actions. Morality goes deeper, restricting our mental behavior. Religious guidelines extend deepest, revealing and judging our fundamental ego-centeredness. We can't hide the karmic hindrances in our minds even when we do good and receive praise.

When Shinran said in *Tannisho* that hell is his fixed home, he was evaluating himself on this deepest level. Shinran was not an evil person according to national law or social morality. But when he was illuminated by the light of the boundless compassion of Amitabha Buddha, he had to acknowledge that he wasn't able to attain enlightenment through his personal efforts, through self-power practice. He found that Mara was within him. So he altered the direction of his spiritual logic. He concluded that people who think they're evil and helpless are the main beneficiaries of Amitabha Buddha's compassion. In the next section of *Tannisho* he commented, in Taitetsu Unno's translation:

> Even a good person attains birth in the Pure Land, how much more so the evil person.
>
> But the people of the world constantly say, even the evil person attains birth, how much more so the good person. Although this appears to be sound at first glance, it goes against the intention of the Primal Vow of Other Power. The reason is that since the person of self-power, being

conscious of doing good, lacks the thought of entrusting himself completely to the Other Power, he isn't the focus of the Primal Vow of Amida. But when he turns over self-power and entrusts himself to Other Power, he attains birth in the land of True Fulfillment.

The Primal Vow was established out of deep compassion for us who cannot become freed from the bondage of birth-and-death through any religious practice, due to the abundance of blind passion. Since its basic intention is to effect the enlightenment of such an evil one, the evil person who entrusts himself to Other Power is truly the one who attains birth in the Pure Land. Thus, even the good person attains birth, how much more so the evil person!

In his childhood, when Sawaki Roshi lived with his adoptive parents in extremely difficult conditions, he sometimes visited a nearby Pure Land temple and listened to the sermons. He also practiced nembutsu, reciting the name of Amitabha Buddha. When he resolved to escape his parents and become a Buddhist monk, he confided his decision to a Pure Land priest he knew. The priest advised, "If you want to become a monk, go to a Zen temple. Because Zen monks often don't have families, they can devote themselves to study, practice, and helping others."

That was why Sawaki Roshi went to Eiheiji. In his teachings, we see the influence of Pure Land Buddhism. An example is his saying: "The calmer we become, the more clearly we see how terrible we are." In our zazen, we see the subtle defilement hidden within the deepest layer of our consciousness. Zazen is not a method to attain enlightenment and become great. Rather our zazen is itself repentance, through which we are illuminated by the boundless light of Buddha. Dogen Zenji expressed this way of living without separation between self and others as "total function."

Considered closely connected with the Lotus Sutra, Kanfugen-bosatsugyohokyo says:

> The ocean of all karmic hindrances
> arises solely from delusive thoughts.

If you wish to make repentance,
sit upright and be mindful of the true reality.
All misdemeanors are like frost and dew,
The sun of wisdom enables them to melt away.

47.

Zazen and Delusion

KODO SAWAKI:
When a husband and wife are in the middle of a quarrel, neither partner thinks they're fighting based on their delusions. However, when they practice zazen, they can understand clearly that they quarreled because of their delusive thoughts.

KOSHO UCHIYAMA:
I once saw a very interesting cartoon by Katsuko Igari in the college cartoon contest sponsored by the *Asahi* newspaper. With all his might, Adam is trying to vomit what he has eaten. At his side, Eve is looking at him anxiously, saying, "Adam, hasn't the apple you ate before come up yet?"

If Sawaki Roshi had seen this cartoon, he would have said, "Zazen is the posture in which we vomit the apple we ate before." When Roshi refers to "the apple we ate before," he doesn't mean the apple eaten by the first man in the ancient time of the myth. He means that when we quarrel, we eat the apple in the form of our dispute. That is, we always find the *I* within our delusive thoughts arising moment by moment. When we act with this hardened *I* and confront each other, we repeatedly eat the apple of original sin.

Although we are almost always living based on delusion, we don't think our thoughts are delusive; we live without even considering this possibility. Why? Because we're completely immersed in delusive thoughts, we treat them as if they were real.

When we do zazen and settle down, we clearly see how we're dominated by delusion. Zazen is indeed the posture of "God, be merciful to me, a sinner!" (Luke 18:13). In our zazen we realize the illusory nature of thoughts, and no matter how powerful they might be, we don't chase after them, try to get rid of them, or act on them. So zazen is the posture of "We know that our old self was crucified with him" (Romans 6:6) or "I have been crucified with Christ" (Galatians 2:19). In the end, zazen is the purest expression of "Be still, and know that I am God!" (Psalms 46:10).

SHOHAKU OKUMURA:
Here, *delusory thought* means thinking based on separation, discrimination, or duality. Of course some thoughts are closer to reality and others might be closer to fantasy, but no thoughts are reality itself. There are good and bad thoughts, but good and bad are based on our discrimination. Transcending such discriminations and living in reality itself is being illuminated by the ultimate light of Buddha. This is the true meaning of religion according to Sawaki Roshi and Uchiyama Roshi. On this point Uchiyama Roshi felt that Pure Land Buddhism and Christianity were not different from Zen.

Vomiting the apple means seeing the delusory nature of our thoughts and letting them go, as we do in zazen. If we feel we're becoming enlightened, that's delusion.

The sentence Uchiyama Roshi quotes from Luke is part of Jesus Christ's sermon in Luke 18:10–14:

> Two men went up to the temple to pray, one a Pharisee and the other a tax collector. The Pharisee, standing by himself, was praying thus, "God, I thank you that I am not like other people: thieves, rogues, adulterers, or even like this tax collector. I fast twice a week; I give a tenth of all my income." But the tax collector, standing far off, would not even look up to heaven, but was beating his breast and saying, "God, be merciful to me, a sinner!" I tell you, this man went down to his home justified rather than the other; for all who exalt themselves will be humbled, but all who humble themselves will be exalted.

In this teaching, we see the same logic as Shinran's "Even a good person attains birth in the Pure Land, how much more so the evil person." Uchiyama Roshi points out that this is the nature of true and universal religion. When Dogen Zenji titled his manual of zazen *Universal Recommendation of Zazen*, or *Fukanzazengi*, he expressed the nature of his zazen practice as a true and universal religion, rather than a practice aimed at producing a select number of enlightened elite.

48.

Spectator Zen

KODO SAWAKI:

There's a famous story from the Taisho period, or 1912–26, that Kubutsu Ohtani gave a ten-thousand-yen tip to a geisha. Yet he wrote the haiku: "How gracious! The Ancestor lived for ninety years wearing paper clothes." This haiku is good, but how could a man who gave a ten-thousand-yen tip compose such a poem? I don't like poets when they lie.

KOSHO UCHIYAMA:

During the Taisho period, ten thousand yen was much more than today; it was almost a man's entire fortune. Although I was just a boy at the time, I heard the stories of Kubutsu Ohtani's extravagant life. I suppose he forgot that a monk should be a beggar from head to toe. Yet he liked to show off his appreciation of his Ancestor's devoted religious life of poverty and austerity.

The tea ceremony should be a practice of *wabi* and *sabi*, of the acceptance of transience and imperfection. Yet these days, the original spirit has been lost and the ceremony has become a play at wabi-sabi. If we consider the ceremony an art or hobby taught at finishing school, it might not matter. But it's not permissible to take such an attitude toward our religious life. Religion should be practiced in our daily lives and not be something that is just "appreciated" from a distance.

However, for human beings, practice is much too tiresome. We want to show our appreciation like sightseers, without doing it ourselves. Like spectator sports, which are very popular, the Zen fad is really a spectator Zen or Zen sightseeing fad.

People have stereotypes of Zen masters as being large-hearted, flexible, straightforward, and natural, like characters in a book. With this image, people go sightseeing in Zen temples and say, "These temples are so beautiful with their simplicity and cleanliness." Such people are only appreciating the art and atmosphere. Needless to say, they have nothing to do with practicing religion as their own lives.

 KODO SAWAKI:
Hey! Why are you looking around at others? This is about you!

SHOHAKU OKUMURA:
The Ancestor Shinran was the first Japanese Buddhist monk who publicly married and had a family. He devoted his life to teaching Pure Land Buddhism in poverty. Most of his community was in the eastern part of Japan, where he spent a few decades. When he was about sixty, he returned to Kyoto and focused on writing and practicing with a small number of followers until he passed away at ninety. His burial place was Honganji, which was then relatively small. Later, in the fifteenth century, Honganji became a large and powerful religious order that maintained a military and fought with warring lords. When the Tokugawa Shogunate government was established in the seventeenth century, Honganji was divided into two branches: East and West. Shin Buddhism remains the largest Buddhist school in Japan.

At both East and West Honganji, the abbots have been descendants of Shinran. In the Meiji era, Shinran's descendants started to use their family name, Ohtani. Koen Ohtani (1875–1943) became the twenty-third abbot of East Honganji at thirty-three; Kubutsu was his pen name as a poet.

The Ohtani family had close relations with the imperial family and other nobility. Kubutsu himself was a count, belonging to the third rank of the aristocracy. He was not only the head of the large religious order but also a businessman. In the Taisho era, he had great authority, power, and wealth. He was a good example of the heavenly beings on earth discussed in chapter 41. Sawaki Roshi introduces an anecdote that shows how extravagant his life was. But later his business failed and East Honganji suffered a financial crisis. Because of this, Kubutsu had to resign from the abbacy in 1925, when he was fifty.

Kubutsu enjoyed religious authority as head of a large order, social status as an aristocrat, and great wealth, yet as a poet he wrote haiku praising Shinran's austere spiritual life. Few can live a life quite as heavenly as Kubutsu's, yet many of us like to "appreciate" the spiritual life of simplicity without actually living it.

49.

Zazen Is Good for Nothing

KODO SAWAKI:

What is zazen good for? Nothing! We should be made to hear this good-for-nothingness so often that we get calluses on our ears and practice good-for-nothing zazen without any expectation. Otherwise, our practice really is good for nothing.

KOSHO UCHIYAMA:

Throughout his life, Sawaki Roshi said, "Zazen is good for nothing." In 1941, I was ordained and became one of his disciples. Soon after, while walking with him, I asked, "I am such a timid person. If I study under your guidance and practice zazen with you for many years until you pass away, can I become even a little bit stronger?" He immediately replied, "No, you can't. No matter how hard and how long you practice, zazen is good for nothing. I didn't become who I am as a result of zazen. By nature I was this kind of person. On this point I haven't changed at all."

As you know, Sawaki Roshi was bighearted, freespirited, and witty, and yet careful and focused. He embodied the image of the ancient Zen master. When I heard his response I thought, "Although Roshi says so with his mouth, if I continue to practice zazen, I must be able to become a better person." With such an expectation, I served him and continued zazen practice until he died.

He passed away on December 21 last year. We'll mark the first anniversary of his death soon. Lately I've been reflecting on my past, and I now understand that zazen really is good for nothing. I'm still a coward and never became even a little bit like Sawaki Roshi.

Finally I came to a conclusion. A violet blooms as a violet and a rose blooms as a rose. For violets, there's no need to desire to become roses.

KODO SAWAKI:
Each of us has our own particular karmic attributes, but it's important that we're all led by Buddha. *Shinjin-datsuraku*, dropping off body and mind, means that we discard our stubborn self-centeredness, trust the Buddha's teaching, and walk following Buddha.

SHOHAKU OKUMURA:
I began to read Uchiyama Roshi's and Sawaki Roshi's books as a high school student. Sawaki Roshi's teaching "zazen is good for nothing" appealed to me very much. In Japanese society, especially in school, we were always asked to be good at something; everything had to be good for something else. Parents, teachers, and the whole society asked us to study hard, get good grades, go to a good university, get a good job, make a good income, and acquire a good car, a good house—and a good coffin. As a teenager, I began to question society's criteria for good and bad.

To find the answer I read many books on history, philosophy, religion, science, and so on. I didn't find a satisfactory answer to the question of the meaning of life. Whatever I read seemed to be one person's idea from their limited experiences in a certain time and society. I wanted to know the meaning of meaning. Finally I decided meaning is meaningless, and therefore human life has no meaning.

And yet human beings cannot live without seeking meaning. When I do something, I have to believe it has some point. I became tired of this circle of seeking meaning and finding meaninglessness. This was the condition in which I encountered Sawaki Roshi's teaching. To stop looking for meaning and simply do good-for-nothing zazen seemed like liberation from that endless circle of a dog chasing its tail.

I wholeheartedly practiced zazen for about ten years at Antaiji and Pioneer Valley Zendo in Massachusetts. I was happy during that time. But after I turned thirty, my body began to break down from the hard labor of building Pioneer Valley in the woods. I had no income and couldn't get medical treatment, so I had to return to Japan.

When I returned there, I couldn't practice in my old way; I had no place to practice and no sangha to practice with. I felt my life was a failure and I was truly a good-for-nothing person. I asked myself, "If zazen is good for nothing, why should it matter if I can't do it?" In the end, I found my zazen hadn't really been good for nothing. Because I practiced good-for-nothing zazen with devotion, I felt my life was justified. Yet this intensity of practice was possible only when I was young, strong, and healthy. In this way I discovered arrogance in a deep layer of my mind.

One day around that time, I found myself sitting zazen alone. There was no need for me to sit formally since I lived without any fellow practitioners. Yet when I sat I experienced a deep peace. And I felt for the first time that I could sit true good-for-nothing zazen. To practice such good-for-nothing zazen isn't easy.

Meaning isn't an absolute, objective truth decided before we're born. Rather, when we begin to do something, like birds flying or fish swimming, help and meaning appear within us and in response to our activity, a meeting of ourselves and all beings.

Uchiyama Roshi's expression "A violet blooms as a violet and a rose blooms as a rose" came from the famous Catholic nun Therese of Lisieux, who called herself a "little flower" and her practice "the little way." Although she felt herself small compared with great saints, she found in this smallness the source of joy.

50

Changeable Mind

KODO SAWAKI:
Sometimes we think a person's behavior is likable, and other times we dislike the same behavior. The same sun rises and sets on New Year's Eve and New Year's Day.

KOSHO UCHIYAMA:
When a man falls in love with a woman, even her flaws look beautiful. Whatever she does seems lovely and elegant to him. But after he begins married life, he gradually tires of her habitual behavior. He watches her and thinks, "Now she's going to do this, and then she'll do that." She does exactly as he expects, and he feels disgusted and can't tolerate her. As his point of view toward her begins to change, her point of view toward him starts changing as well. This is a problem.

In such a crisis, if the two are merely physically mature but emotionally childish, their relationship will collapse. They used up all their affection as lovers and honeymooners. As a result of their selfishness, with the excuse of incompatibility, they'll have affairs or divorce.

To be more than merely sexually infatuated, to truly love a person, is very difficult. Romantic love is ecstasy and intoxication, but marriage is a long voyage. We must rise above and go through millions of waves—the waves in our own minds. If we drift along acting on each and every wave, we'll easily sink.

To live a religious life of zazen as the stability of our lives is to thoroughly see that our minds are always changing, and we must find a steadfast way to live without being dragged around by our thoughts.

On New Year's Eve and New Year's Day, the sun rises exactly the same, but we see it in an altered frame of mind. When we feel at a dead end, we should see the difficulties are merely in our thoughts, refresh ourselves, and welcome a new day.

KODO SAWAKI:

If the skin on our head is too thick, like a pomelo's, nothing can enter. If our thinking is too rigid, like a soldier's, we can't be relaxed and flexible. Life must be vital and flexible.

SHOHAKU OKUMURA:

In Japan, until the solar calendar was adopted at the end of the nineteenth century, we counted age using traditional East Asian reckoning. At birth we are one year old. On the next New Year's Day, we turn two. Everyone becomes a year older on New Year's Day. If someone is born December 31, the next day they turn two. Therefore, we didn't have the custom of celebrating individual birthdays; New Year's Day was everyone's birthday. Probably that's one of the reasons New Year's Day was the most important celebration in Japan.

This feeling continues today. Before New Year's Eve, families thoroughly clean their homes. They prepare feasts for the first three days of the New Year. At midnight on New Year's Eve, people visit Buddhist temples to ring the bell 108 times to usher out the old year, reflecting on its events and letting them go. The next day, they visit Shinto shrines to mark a fresh start and pray for fortune in the coming year.

One of the important customs in celebrating New Year's Day is honoring the year's first sunrise. So sunrise on New Year's Day has special resonance for many Japanese. Some climb Mount Fuji or other sacred mountains to pay tribute to this sunrise.

It seems to me that Sawaki Roshi and Uchiyama Roshi use this example with slightly different meanings. Sawaki Roshi means that the sun rises in the same way 365 days a year, but our minds are in different modes on New Year's Eve and New Year's Day. This is an example of the changeability of our minds. Uchiyama Roshi says it's important to refresh our minds by letting go of our thoughts instead of getting tangled in them, just as we make a fresh start on New Year's Day.

Sawaki Roshi's final statement in this chapter means that if our mind lacks sensitivity and we think nothing matters, we cannot live harmoniously with others. Yet if our mind is rigidly set and we think everything should be done a particular way, our lives cannot be flexible.

51.

A Rose Is a Rose

KODO SAWAKI:

To practice the buddha way is not to let our minds wander but to become one with what we're doing. This is called *zanmai* (or *samadhi*) and *shikan* (or "just doing").

Eating rice isn't preparation for shitting; shitting isn't preparation for making manure. And yet these days people think that high school is preparation for college and college is preparation for a good job.

KOSHO UCHIYAMA:

Many parents bribe and pressure their children to get good grades or pass the entrance exams, saying, "Study hard! Study hard!" Furthermore they blatantly push their children into the realm of *asura*, the fighting spirits: "Don't be shut out by others! Beat them and go to the top school!" If they think this is an expression of enthusiasm for their children's education, they're making a big mistake. If their children are smart they'll find it ridiculous to study in competition with others. If their children are timid, they'll become daunted and neurotic. Only foolish and unaware children follow their parents' and teachers' "advice."

If I were a teacher, I'd say:

> You don't need to get good grades. It's not necessary to go to a famous school. Just do things naturally and straight-forwardly. As a violet, it's enough to bloom as a violet. As a rose, it's fine to bloom as a rose. It's meaningless for a violet

to think being a violet isn't good enough, that you should work hard to produce a rose.

However, if a violet doesn't become a violet, you spoil your life force. This is absurd. Try to express your life force to the fullest. You want to know whether you're a violet or a rose? I don't know, and you don't need to know. Life is possibility; it's not fixed. You don't need to decide what you are—just live your self and naturally bloom your own flower.

Instead of studying to get good grades, you should bloom as the flower of this time here and now, because this is the time to study. If you're sleeping, reading comic books, or eating lunch during class, you can't bloom the flower of this time of studying. Open your eyes wide to read the textbook, and listen carefully to the teacher.

SHOHAKU OKUMURA:

In chapter 49, Uchiyama Roshi compared himself to a violet and Sawaki Roshi to a rose. And he said that's fine. Here he says students don't need to worry about whether they're roses or violets. They should simply bloom their own flowers. To do this, they need to strive to manifest their life force to the best of their ability moment by moment.

Therese of Lisieux wrote, in John Clarke's translation:

Jesus deigned to teach me this mystery. He set before me the book of nature; I understood how all the flowers He has created are beautiful, how the splendor of the rose and the whiteness of the lily do not take away the perfume of the little violet or the delightful simplicity of the daisy. I understood that if all flowers wanted to be roses, nature would lose her springtime beauty, and the fields would no longer be decked out with little wild flowers.

Soto Zen monk and poet Ryokan (1758–1831) wrote a poem that echoes Therese of Lisieux:

Within a begging bowl,
Putting violets and dandelions together
I offer them to
All buddhas in the three times.

Violets and dandelions are small and without market value, and yet in
the spring they decorate the fields beautifully. While Ryokan was begging, he picked these flowers with children, put them in his begging
bowl, and offered them to the buddhas. Little flowers like violets can
be a priceless offering to the buddhas.

Of course, luxurious roses can be an offering too. They can also
easily be the objects of human desire caused by the three poisonous
minds: greed, anger, and delusion.

Uchiyama Roshi encourages young people to be mindful and
bloom their own lives, small or big, moment by moment.

52

Corruption and Rudeness

KODO SAWAKI:

In Buddhadharma, defilement is defined as the most revolting attitude. When a company president or executive behaves as if they're important, that's defilement. When this defilement is cleansed, our practice is shikan—just doing.

KOSHO UCHIYAMA:

On an evening several days before the first anniversary of Sawaki Roshi's death, a resident student at Antaiji informed me of the arrival of a visiting priest. When I went to the entrance, Taiko Furukawa Roshi, archbishop of the Myoshinji sect, was standing there. I greeted him and invited him to my room. Furukawa Roshi said, "I've already visited the Buddha hall and paid homage to Sawaki Roshi's relics. I must go now." Filled with awe, I saw him off.

Shortly after Sawaki Roshi retired to Antaiji, Furukawa Roshi had visited to inquire about his health. After Sawaki Roshi had passed away, Furukawa Roshi made two condolence calls to offer incense. At his second call, I wasn't able to meet him because I was out on an errand, and I hadn't written a letter of apology. This was very rude to such a high-ranking person. A small and poor temple like Antaiji and the abbot of the great Rinzai monastery Myoshinji do not fit well together. In fact when he first proposed visiting, I hesitated, saying there was no suitable place at Antaiji for an archbishop to be seated. But after I met him, I admired his down-to-earth and virtuous character, undefiled by his high status.

At the same time, I also admired the innocence of my student.

When I told him, "That was the archbishop. You should let me know as soon as he arrives," the student responded naively, "What's an archbishop?" I was sorry to be the most defiled person among the three of us.

However, in the Zen tradition, there's a saying: "A high place is high level, a low place is low level." If we're too idealistic, we become rude and cause confusion in society. We should intend to be free of discrimination as an ideal, but we can't avoid being somewhat worldly. We need to live in this human world and make repentance for the compromise involved.

KODO SAWAKI:

If we don't understand differences, we're foolish; if we're caught up in differences, we're mediocre human beings trapped by our worldly judgments.

SHOHAKU OKUMURA:

Defilement is a translation of *zenna*, an important expression in Dogen's teaching. Originally it appeared in a dialogue between the Sixth Ancestor, Huineng (638–713), and his disciple Nanyue Huairang (Nangaku Ejo, 677–744).

> When Huairang visited the Ancestor for the first time, Huineng asked, "Where are you from?"
> Huairang answered that he came from a certain place.
> Then Huineng asked, "What is it that thus comes?"
> Huairang didn't understand.
> After eight years of practice with Huineng, Huairang finally understood the question and visited Huineng again.
> Huineng asked, "How do you understand it?"
> Huairang replied, "If I say something, I am off the mark."
> Huineng asked, "If so, is there practice and verification?"
> Huairang said, "We cannot say there is not practice and verification, but we cannot defile them."
> Then Huineng said, "This nondefilement is what all the ancestors have protected and maintained. You should carefully maintain it."

In "Bendowa," Dogen said, "We must know that in order not to allow defilement of enlightenment inseparable from practice, the buddha ancestors vigilantly teach us not to slacken practice." If we practice with desire to gain something, that's defilement. And if we're proud of our practice and its results, that's also defilement. We need to just practice free of such defilement.

Taiko Furukawa Roshi (1871–1968) was the twenty-second archbishop of the Myoshinji sect of the Rinzai School. Myoshinji was established by Kanzan Egen (1277–1361) in 1337. It's one of the largest Rinzai monasteries in Kyoto, and the head temple of about 3,400 temples. When he visited Sawaki Roshi in 1964, Furukawa Roshi was ninety-three.

"A high place is high level, a low place is low level" comes from a koan:

> Yangshan was digging on a hillside to make a rice paddy. He said, "This place is so low, that place is so high."
>
> Guishan said, "Water makes things equal. Why don't you level it with water?"
>
> Yangshan said, "Water is not reliable, teacher. A high place is high level. A low place is low level."
>
> Guishan agreed.

Dogen quotes this saying in "Tenzokyokun," or "Instructions for the Cook," in *Dogen's Pure Standards*:

> After preparing the breakfast vegetables, get together the wooden rice container, pots, and utensils that were used at lunch for the rice and soup, and attentively wash them clean. For all the various things, put away in high places things that belong in high places, and put away in low places things that belong in low places. A high place is high level and low place is low level.

53.

Fabrication

KODO SAWAKI:

We human beings always have some calcified ideas. To believe some kind of "ism" means we're addicted to particular ideas. Because of such fixed views, we cannot see Buddhadharma even though it's very close to us.

All thoughts are based on solidified views; Buddhadharma is prior to such views being formed.

KOSHO UCHIYAMA:

Sawaki Roshi took great pains his entire life to talk about Buddhadharma in vivid everyday language. He always said, "The wild boys at the Fifth High School who came to practice with me in Kumamoto didn't let me continue being an old-fashioned Buddhist priest. They forced me to speak without worn-out Buddhist expressions." When I talk with young students, if I bring up technical terms or quotes from scriptures, they immediately yawn. If I ignore this and continue to talk in such a boring way, they won't come back. This is very interesting.

After all, Buddhist terms and scriptures are merely enumerations of jargon. Such language only talks about other people's thoughts using those people's expressions. The young students sensitively perceive that the vigorous life force of the speaker is not manifested in such talk. I think Japanese Buddhism has completely lost energy because priests speak in too conceptual and dogmatic a way. Although not as overly conceptual as Buddhism, today's various "isms" and ideologies are solidified views based on dogmatized human thoughts.

On the contrary, Buddhadharma in its original form is not a fabrication of human thought. We should discover the self in the reality of life prior to thought, and we should act based on this life force. From ancient times, teachers have said that we shouldn't be fixed in our views about Buddha and Dharma. This means that to practice Buddhadharma is to allow our life force, here and now, to flow freely and vigorously without being caught up in any "ism," including Buddhism.

SHOHAKU OKUMURA:
Sawaki Roshi practiced as the instructor at Daijiji in Kumamoto from 1916 to 1921. Daijiji is one of the oldest Soto Zen temples and was founded by Dogen Zenji's disciple Kangan Giin (1217–1300). Sotan Oka Roshi was appointed as abbot, but he couldn't live there. He invited Sawaki Roshi to serve as instructor of the training monks. While at Daijiji, Sawaki Roshi was invited to speak at the Fifth High School. The students were moved and some of them came to Daijiji to practice. Sawaki Roshi was invited to give monthly talks at the school for several years. Many students were influenced by him, and their connection continued over the years.

This high school was one of eight established by the government. Students of these schools were guaranteed to enter one of the seven imperial universities without an entrance exam, so they were considered elite. They didn't need to study hard to get good marks. They had a lot of time to study things outside class.

This was during the Taisho era (1912–26), which followed the Meiji era (1868–1912). During the Meiji period, Japan focused on studying Western civilization and experienced a lot of war. During the Taisho, other than World War I, Japan didn't fight much and was relatively stable and prosperous. In those days, Japanese people were confident they had become equal to Western countries in military and economic power. They began to recover their appreciation for traditional Japanese culture. Politically there was a movement called "Taisho democracy," which reflected the rise of the two-party system. On the other hand, socialism, communism, and anarchism were introduced to Japan. These contradicted the imperial system.

Young people were the most sensitive both to these novel ideas and the renewed appreciation of traditional culture. They asked Sawaki Roshi to read Western philosophy, socialism, and Marxism, and they often came to his temple to debate. While Sawaki Roshi's Zen practice influenced these students, he in turn was influenced by his discussions with them. These youths later became politicians, government officials, scholars, schoolteachers, doctors, and so on, and continued to support Sawaki Roshi.

Even after he died in 1965, some of those who practiced with him in the early decades of the century came to sit sesshin at Antaiji. They were then in their seventies or eighties. At that time, the majority of training monks and visiting practitioners under the guidance of Uchiyama Roshi were young people my age, the so-called baby boomers. We were critical of everything before World War II, including those elders, because they hadn't opposed the war.

54

Grading Morality

KODO SAWAKI:
Someone asked a mathematician, "Does the number 1 really exist?" The answer was that mathematics assumes the number exists, and everything else is built on that assumption. In Buddhism, as Seng-can's "Xinxinming" says, the number 1 does not exist: "Two exists depending on one. Do not cling even to oneness. . . . One is all; all is one."

KOSHO UCHIYAMA:
I've heard that computers calculate quickly and give us an exact answer. Last year, the bill for my national health insurance was awfully big. I thought this must be a mistake and asked them to check. They said it seemed the computer operator had input one or two extra digits. I was impressed that the computer revealed the official's mistake so quickly and exactly.

The other day, a middle-school teacher visited me and said, "I have a headache: we have to evaluate the students' sense of responsibility and morality. If you were a schoolteacher, what would you do?" Since I don't know anything about today's schools, I was surprised. I understand quantification in the sciences but I don't think it reasonable to quantify the life of human beings. I think the sense of responsibility of the officials at the Ministry of Education who ordered schoolteachers to grade such a thing should be evaluated. They deserve the lowest mark.

I'm sorry the schoolteacher has to follow such a ridiculous order. I told him, "If I were you, I'd give every student a 90. There's a Zen saying: 'Perfect completeness should be avoided.' So instead of 100, I'd give a 90. Then, separate from the grading, I'd discuss the topic of responsibility in a way understandable to the students. Finally I'd say, 'Both of us should try to live in such a way.'"

KODO SAWAKI:

Without doubt, things should be done a certain way, and yet everything is fine. There's no fixed rule to follow, but we should act in the best way for each situation.

SHOHAKU OKUMURA:

An *axiom* is used as a premise of reasonable thinking in mathematics and logic. Unless we accept axioms without doubt, we can't think rationally. That is, rational thought rests on acceptance without evidence. Our thinking is supported only by assumptions taken for granted. These assumptions themselves aren't supported by anything. Yet without acceptance, we can't participate in human activities. Faith is necessary not only for religion but for all of life.

Without setting a fixed origin and axes, we can't measure position or movement. Even in everyday activities, we assume an origin and X and Y axes. On both axes, positive and negative exist. For example, the X axis could represent whether I should do something, and the Y axis whether I want to. An action could be what I should do and want to do (+,+), what I should do and yet don't want to (+,-), what I shouldn't do but want to (-, +), or what I shouldn't do and don't want to (-,-). When we face things and consider whether to take action or not, we automatically make the origin and axes, gauging the situation. If the result is entirely positive (+,+), we take action without hesitation. Otherwise, we have to consider carefully.

However, one flaw in this way of thinking is that the origin can shift within time and space. Depending whether I live in Japan, the U.S., or another country, whether I live in a Buddhist, Christian, Islamic, or other culture, and whether I'm a young, rebellious person or an old, conservative person, the origin and axes are different.

To quantify human actions today, we often use money as the yardstick. Activities that make money are worthwhile; others are a waste. This system might work in the world of finance. But these days even spiritual practice is judged in economic terms: if it doesn't generate income, it isn't considered important. Money is the most common yardstick, and we think it's objective, but it's not very useful for measuring quality. Restaurants serving junk food and gourmet food can both make a lot of money.

55.

Self-Centered Motivation

KODO SAWAKI:
Doing good can be bad. Some people do good to make themselves look good.

KOSHO UCHIYAMA:
Suppose someone visits people in long-term care with gifts, saying, "I'd like to help you receive medical care and recuperate as comfortably as possible." Then he runs for political office and during his campaign he says, "Nice to meet you! I'm a supporter of patients throughout the country. If I win, I'll work to construct better facilities for you." He wins and becomes a politician. While he works to establish facilities for patients, he takes kickbacks and lines his own pockets. Is he a supporter of the patients or does he prey on them? This is a very delicate question. I regret that this is often the way of society. We should judge ourselves by ourselves, as if we were standing alone before God on Judgment Day.

In Japan right now, we're disappointed with the government because there's hardly anyone who devotes their wealth to politics, as in the Meiji and early Taisho eras. Now most politicians use their political activities to increase their personal holdings. Religion's the same.

Depending whether we believe in religion for personal profit or let go of this gaining mind for the sake of faith, the meaning of our practice changes completely. The former is a heretic who exploits God or Buddha, while the latter is a truly religious person. When someone prostrates before God or Buddha and prays devoutly, it's impossible to tell from the outside whether his faith is true or false. It depends whether we're seeking benefit for ourselves, others, or Buddha. Even a holy person respected by many could be driven by a subtly selfish motive.

KODO SAWAKI:
We must all reflect on our motivations with eyes wide open. Somehow before we know it, we're playing to the gallery, anxious about our popularity like an entertainer. If our practice is a performance for an audience, it cannot be Buddhadharma.

SHOHAKU OKUMURA:
This chapter again addresses defilement in the deepest layer of the mind.

Intentionally or not, we may create unwholesome karma even when doing good. We must carefully examine our motivations. Identifying twisted karma is easier when we take unwholesome actions that disturb others than when we're trying to help; even if we fail to recognize our bad behavior at the time, other people will let us know through their advice, blame, anger, or dislike. But when we create twisted karma with our good deeds, people are usually happy and praise us, and we in turn are proud of our actions. In these cases, perceiving the deep and subtle self-centeredness within our benevolence can be very difficult. This is why our practice of zazen as repentance is significant. In zazen, we cannot hide from ourselves. As the Kanfugenbosatsugyohokyo says, "If you wish to make repentance, sit upright and be mindful of the true reality."

For a few years in my thirties, I supported my practice by begging. I lived at a small temple as a caretaker, sat zazen, and had a five-day sesshin each month with a few people. I also worked on translating Dogen Zenji's and Uchiyama Roshi's books from Japanese to English. I begged a few times a month, raising barely enough to pay for health insurance, utilities, telephone, and food.

While begging, I sometimes felt guilty. People donated without knowing who I was or what I was doing. They simply trusted my Buddhist robes. The source of my guilt was that I couldn't do anything in return for those who supported my life and practice. My zazen and translation didn't contribute anything to their lives. Japanese people don't need to read English translations of Buddhist texts.

Once when I was begging, a boy about ten said to me, "You want money, don't you?" This question became my koan. I couldn't say no because when I begged I hoped to receive money to support my life and practice. But if money were what I really wanted, I wouldn't beg; I knew more efficient and easier ways to make money.

I believed I was doing zazen and translation for the sake of Dharma, not for my personal benefit, but I didn't know whether anyone would want to read Zen texts translated into English by a Japanese practitioner who was neither a scholar nor a professional translator. I had to examine my motivation. Was this way of life truly for the Dharma or merely to support activities based on my personal preferences?

Now, thirty years later, some people appreciate my work, so I can say that what I was doing back then had some benefit, but at the time I couldn't know. Actually my motives were mixed: I hoped my work would benefit people, and I also liked it. The important point is to keep investigating one's motivations. Judging oneself is very difficult; we easily believe our motives are good, and we can even become intoxicated with our good intentions. But in zazen we let go of that belief too—that we're good. We just do what we're doing for its own sake.

56

Seamless Practice

KODO SAWAKI:

Human life is complicated. There are times of war when fire-bombs fall from the sky and times of peace when we can take a mid-day nap by the fireplace. Sometimes we have to work all night, and sometimes we can enjoy drinking sake. Buddhadharma is living this life of ever-changing circumstances following the Buddha's teachings.

KOSHO UCHIYAMA:

The sword master Musashi Miyamoto, it's said, never took a bath because while bathing he would be defenseless. If we want to polish our skills to the utmost and truly become a master of a certain art, we must have strong willpower and rigorous training, as Musashi did. But for us common people, it's not possible to go through such training.

Some people try hard to practice zazen, thinking that Zen is a discipline for strengthening their willpower and skill. Their practice may become a masterful performance, but such training cannot be called a universal religion that can be practiced by anyone.

Sawaki Roshi always taught us to be attentive without *suki*, without break, but he didn't mean that one could never take a bath! He taught attentiveness to our everyday lives, including stormy and calm days, always guided by the Buddha.

The other day, someone visited me and asked, "I wish to practice zazen under your guidance. But because I live far away, I can't come to Antaiji very often. I'd like to practice zazen at home. What should I keep in mind to avoid doing zazen in a mistaken way?" I responded,

"If your wife and children say, 'Daddy has become nicer since he began to do zazen,' then your practice is on the right track."

KODO SAWAKI:

There's often a person who thinks that he alone is right, even though he's disliked by everyone in his family. You're not right as long as you think that only you are right. A practitioner who prides himself on being enlightened but is avoided by his family has missed the mark.

SHOHAKU OKUMURA:

Musashi Miyamoto (1584–1645) is still one of the most popular heroes of samurai novels and movies in modern Japan. In one story, he was attacked while taking a bath without his weapon. After that, he supposedly never bathed again. I don't believe this is historically true.

Suki is difficult to translate. D. T. Suzuki explained this word in *Zen and Japanese Culture*:

> *Suki* . . . means "a space between two objects," or "a slit or split or crack in one solid object." When continuity is broken up and a crack begins to show, there is a *suki*. When tension slackens, certain signs of laxity appear—which is *suki*. In Takuan's terminology, *suki* corresponds to "stopping." In swordsmanship, this is taken advantage of by the enemy, who is always too ready not to let the opportunity slip away vainly. On one of the self-portraits of Miyamoto Musashi, a great swordsman and painter of the seventeenth century, his pose would indicate him to be full of *suki*, but he keeps his eyes wide open so as not to allow the opponent to make use of the *suki* that is really only apparent. A great deal of spiritual training is needed for a swordsman to reach this stage, properly called "open on all sides."

In the portrait D. T. Suzuki mentions, Musashi's hands hold his long and short swords and are relaxed at his sides. According to Suzuki, this is the final stage of the swordsman, without any defensiveness, and yet the enemy cannot attack. When Musashi was young, he was always totally defended; only when he was truly mature could he achieve openness, thanks to his rigorous training.

Uchiyama Roshi says that "being without suki" is different from the common use of this expression as relaxing one's guard. In Uchiyama Roshi's usage, it means being continuously attentive to every situation in our lives. When we need to work, we wholeheartedly work; when we can take a nap, simply take a nap; when we bathe, just relax and enjoy. We can live our complex lives following the Buddha's teachings in every moment.

57.

Dogen Zenji's Appeal

KODO SAWAKI:
One of the reasons Dogen Zenji appeals to me is that he sees Buddhadharma as the way to live the self. He doesn't think Buddhism is a fairy tale to make people feel better about life.

KOSHO UCHIYAMA:
When I first read Dogen Zenji's writing, I was most impressed by his saying, "To study the buddha way is to study the self." From the age of sixteen or seventeen, I had been questioning the meaning of life. To find the answer, I studied Western philosophy and Christian theology. After all this studying, I finally encountered Dogen Zenji's work and resolved to become a monk in his tradition. I was most fortunate to be able to study under the guidance of Sawaki Roshi, who had a modern perspective and admired Dogen Zenji because he starts from the self.

Now I can see the truth in Christianity and Pure Land Buddhism. But I think it was natural that I couldn't accept them when I was young; they seemed to require a belief in the redemption of our sins through the cross or in salvation by Amitabha's vow. I couldn't see how they related to my life. If, negating our intelligence and powers of reason, we have to believe stories about the past merely because they're written in the Bible or Buddhist scriptures, then we must also believe the legends in books about immortal mountain wizards.

Such reasoning shows my skeptical, argumentative tendency. We modern people cannot help saying, "Because intelligence is also a function of the self, we shouldn't deny it and just believe something.

Such belief cannot be the truth of the self." This perspective must be frustrating to many traditional religions, which probably view people today as very stubborn and ignorant.

However, Dogen Zenji's attitude "To study the buddha way is to study the self" enables skeptical modern people to enter Zen practice. Such teaching resonates with those who aren't endowed with much religious piety. But then he goes further; he helps us see that even though intelligence is one of the abilities of the self, the self is not grasped by intelligence alone. He leads us to the truth of the self that is beyond intelligence—to zazen beyond thinking.

SHOHAKU OKUMURA:

My family has been Buddhist for many generations. But that merely means we have a family grave at a certain temple. We visit a few times a year and attend funeral ceremonies and memorial services. I didn't know anything about Buddhist teachings until high school.

When I became interested in religion because of my questions about life, I tried to read the Buddhist sutra books I found in the drawers of the family altar. One of them, I think, was the Kannongyo, the sutra of Avalokiteshvara. The only thing I understood was that if I chanted Avalokiteshvara's name, all my wishes would be fulfilled. I didn't think that was what I was looking for. Because Shinran's *Tannisho* was pretty popular, I tried to read it too. But I couldn't accept the basic teaching of Amitabha Buddha's power of salvation. And I didn't understand Shinran's logic that while a good person can be born in the Pure Land, an evil person will even more easily be born there.

Next, I went to a Christian church and read the Bible. I didn't understand why I had to believe a particular nation's myth of God's creation of the world and how human beings became sinners. I knew that in China and Japan there were other creation myths. Why should I believe one version and negate the others?

If I hadn't happened to read Uchiyama Roshi's book, I probably wouldn't have become interested in any religion. When I read it, I didn't understand what he said about zazen and Buddhist teachings, but I understood that Uchiyama Roshi had the same questions I had about life. And he devoted his life to searching for the answers. After finding them in zazen, he continued to practice and teach younger generations. He was the first person I met who lived that way, and I wanted to live like him. To understand his teaching and practice, I went to a Buddhist university and studied Shakyamuni Buddha's and Dogen Zenji's teachings. I was lucky to encounter these teachings that we can start from studying the self instead of having to believe certain myths.

58

The Value of Things

KODO SAWAKI:

When we're not sick, we forget our bodies. When my legs were strong, I walked and ran, forgetting my feet. Lately, because my legs are getting sick and weak, I begin to appreciate that they're really great things. When we're healthy, we forget our health and just work.

When we think of a certain thing, there's usually something wrong with it. When our mind and its objects do not arise, there's nothing special.

Often people say that my talks aren't miraculous at all. I think this is true. I myself am not sacred. The Buddhadharma simply guides us to the place where there's nothing special.

Many people misunderstand faith as a kind of intoxicated ecstasy. There are exhilarations or illusions that seem holy. True faith appears when we sober up.

KOSHO UCHIYAMA:

What's most essential for life? Many people would reply, "Money!" However, even if we consider the purpose of our lives to be just maintaining our physical bodies, money still isn't most important. First is air, next water, then heat, light, food, and so on. Money should be listed farther down.

Since Japan is blessed with air and water, we completely take them for granted. Air and water must be pure, without particular odor or taste, to nurture living beings. Because these things are essential to us, they become so ordinary that we live without even thinking of them.

As for the mind, what's the highest value? In Buddhism, the most important thing is to manifest our life force in the purest way, without being defiled by the three poisonous minds or blinded by our self-centered views. After all, the Buddhadharma guides us to the place of "nothing special." Living led by the Buddhadharma means living sobered up from all kinds of intoxication.

SHOHAKU OKUMURA:
Sawaki Roshi stopped traveling to teach, and he retired at Antaiji when he was eighty-three. The main reason was a problem with his legs caused by an injury he suffered as a soldier in his early twenties.

"When our mind and its objects do not arise, there's nothing special." In the Sutta Nipata, Shakyamuni Buddha discusses liberation from contact between sense organs and their objects, which is attained by lack of separation into subject and object. According to early Buddhist teachings, such separation between subject and object is the cause of suffering within samsara. Influenced by the wind of ignorance, the mind divides the world into subject and object, with some objects categorized as attractive and others as ordinary or negative. When we study and practice, we often see the Dharma, enlightenment, nirvana, or our practice become objects of our desire, and we create samsara within our practice.

In "Tenzokyokun," which is translated in *Dogen's Pure Standards*, Dogen Zenji quotes a verse by Xuedou:

> One character, three characters, five and seven characters,
> Having thoroughly investigated the ten thousand things,
>   none have any foundation.
> At midnight the white moon sets into the dark ocean.
> When searching for the black dragon's pearl, you will find
>   they are numerous.

Usually we feel that things are always changing, and if only we can find some essence to rely on, our problems will be solved. This poem says that each and every conditioned thing reflects the moon, or pearl, of wholeness. All things are nothing special, yet are also the dragon's treasure. We need to venerate and care for them as the elements of our precious lives.

In their book *Great Fool,* Ryuiichi Abe and Peter Haskel translate Ryokan:

> Walking along
> I followed the drifting stream to its source
> But reaching the headwaters left me stunned
> That's when I realized that the true source isn't a particu-
> lar place you can reach
> So, now, wherever my staff sets down
> I just play in the current's eddies and swirls.

When Ryokan traced the river, he found its origin in a tiny spring. There was nothing special about the source, only the water itself. Eventually this same water flows into a huge river. Although we often think that reaching the spiritual source is enlightenment, in fact no spiritual source exists beyond the branching streams. Nothing special is really the most precious thing.

59.

Habitual Views

KODO SAWAKI:
The "Joyuishikiron," or "Demonstration of Consciousness Only," says that when the inner consciousness evolves, it seems to divide into two parts. Even though only one consciousness arises, it seems to us that subject (I) and objects (the world) exist separately. Within this structure, we start to chase after objects or flee from them. Then we begin to make a great fuss over nothing. Delusive desire is an interesting thing.

KOSHO UCHIYAMA:
I often hear office workers say, "The toughest thing isn't the work itself, but the politics at work." I think it's really true. With work the difficulty is just the amount. If you have a lot, you can get through it by working overtime. But in dealing with coworkers, people who make you nervous or upset are in front of your eyes every day, and you can't change the situation simply through your own efforts.

I think there are various kinds of people who offend us. About some we say, "Everything he does is annoying. He's always sucking up to the boss." Of others: "I feel she's always criticizing me." When we come into contact with people who irritate us every day, eventually we can't stand it any longer and explode with anger, or we hold in our chronic discontent and make ourselves neurotic.

When someone bothers us, we should know that this reaction occurs not simply because such an annoying person exists separately from our consciousness but also because of our habitual and biased way of viewing and evaluating things. We must understand this thoroughly.

Delicious food attracts our attention only because we're hungry. Beautiful people catch our eyes only if we have sexual desire. In other words, only when appetite and desire exist within us does a world responding to those conditions appear outside us. When the inner consciousness (the individual life force called *I*) arises, the world *I* see according to my conditioned consciousness will appear. Then we pursue or avoid various objects that we perceive in this world. Our delusive desire is indeed interesting.

SHOHAKU OKUMURA:

The "Demonstration of Consciousness Only" is one of the most important texts in the Chinese Yogacara School, which was founded by the traveler and translator Xuanzang (in Japanese: Genjo; 602–64). This school was transmitted to Japan in the Nara period and called Hosso-shu. It still exists. Sawaki Roshi studied it thoroughly while at Horyuji for five years. His quote in this chapter expresses one of the fundamental points of consciousness-only theory: all we see, hear, smell, taste, touch, and think is only consciousness. We don't see objects themselves as they are.

Sawaki Roshi's saying, "When the inner consciousness evolves, it seems as if there are two parts," isn't an exact quote. In the original text, there are two similar sentences close to each other. In Francis Cook's translation, the first is "The substance of consciousness evolves to resemble two parts." The next paragraph says, "Internal conscious-ness evolves resembling an external realm." The text continues:

> As a result of the power of impressions (*vasana*) from imag-ining a self and dharmas, when the consciousnesses are born, they change into a self and dharmas. Even though the images of this self and dharmas are within conscious-ness, still, due to imagination, they appear to be external. From beginningless time, sentient beings consider them to be real selves and dharmas as a result of this grasping. One is like a dreamer whose mind, because of the power of

the dream, appears in the form of various external things and who consequently considers them to be really external things.

Since Dogen Zenji became a monk in the Tendai tradition, he probably never studied Yogacara theory. Yogacara and Tendai didn't get along. Tendai considered Yogacara expedient, or second-class, Mahayana. Scholars don't find any quotes from Yogacara texts or expressions in Dogen's writings.

Sawaki Roshi's deep understanding and broad knowledge of Yogacara made his approach unique in the Soto Zen tradition. The teaching of Consciousness Only is the basis of his comments in the next chapter about actuality.

60.

Reality

KODO SAWAKI:
We often confidently say "I saw it with my own eyes" or "I heard it with my own ears," but these eyes and ears are questionable. We're all deceived by our eyes, ears, noses, tongues, bodies, and minds. We talk about whether we're happy or unhappy, but these too are only transitory experiences. In reality, there's nothing special.

KOSHO UCHIYAMA:
A student visited me for the first time and before saying anything else, he asked, "Do you support the emperor system or not?" At that moment I understood that he was a simple-minded fellow who had been infected with right-wing ideology. Nowadays there isn't any necessity for serious arguments about whether we support or refute the emperor system. However, this student thought that this question was the foundation of everything else. Until he determined a person's attitude toward this, he couldn't begin to talk about anything else. That made me laugh.

During the student riots of the sixties and seventies, many people thought that discussing the consequences of the riots was talking about the reality of Japanese society. When the author Yukio Mishima killed himself by harakiri after a failed coup, a lot of people thought that talking about him was talking about reality. Actually, revolutions and wars often develop from overexcited, conditioned views and biased ways of thinking—that is, group stupidity. Such arguments have nothing to do with true reality. How hallucinatory are these ideas about "reality"!

KODO SAWAKI:

Everything is just a dream. "Reality" is only reality within a dream. People think revolutions and wars are astounding, but they're struggles in a dream. When you're dead, you might easily see, "Oh! That was just a dream."

When you dream, it's difficult to know you're dreaming. If you pinch your cheek, you feel pain; this pain is also in the dream. We interact with one another in a dream, so we don't recognize the dream as a dream.

Everybody is in his or her own dream. The divergences among these dreams are the problem.

SHOHAKU OKUMURA:

In Buddhism *dream* is used with at least two meanings. One is the opposite of awakening, meaning delusion. Within delusion, we cannot see that both self and objects are empty, or in the theory of Consciousness Only, one consciousness evolves into an apparent split between subject and objects. We believe that *I* and the environment around *I* exist as we think. And we create our stories of success and failure, ups and downs. Then we live in samsara. This is one meaning of *dream*. Within this kind of dream, we feel our homemade stories are reality.

Another meaning of dream is that when we wake from this delusion, we see the reality of the emptiness of self and things. Then we start to see that our lives in samsara are like a dream, where we are always chasing or escaping something. The end of the Diamond Sutra says, "All conditioned things are like a dream, a phantom, a bubble, or a shadow, like a drop of dew, and also a flash of lightning. We should see them like this." Within our original dream we feel that self and things exist independently; when we awaken from this illusion, we see our sense of separation is the real dream.

There's an interesting story from Zhuang Zhou. Once he dreamed he was a butterfly. He was happily flying and forgot he was Zhuang Zhou. After he woke, he wondered whether he was a man who had dreamed of being a butterfly or a butterfly dreaming of being a man.

An eminent Yogacara monk and scholar, Ryohen (1194–1252), contemporary of Dogen Zenji, wrote in *The Essence of Contemplating Mind, Awakening Dream*, or *Kanjin-kakumu sho*:

> When people within a dream realize they are dreaming, they will awaken from the dream without fail. Now although we are within the dream of life and death, if we repeatedly contemplate the principle that *self* and *objects* are only the productions of our minds, like a dream, we are close to the morning of awakening.

When Sawaki Roshi uses the word *dream*, he points to this Yogacara teaching. In the next five chapters, 61 through 65, Uchiyama Roshi collected Sawaki Roshi's sayings about "the self that is connected with the universe," or the reality of the self we begin to see when we awaken from our dream.

61.

The Self That Is Connected with the Universe

KODO SAWAKI:
We cannot maintain ourselves by ourselves. Rather, when we give up *I*, we become simply the self that is connected with the universe.

KOSHO UCHIYAMA:
In our everyday life, when we want to talk about something, we talk about it. When we want to go somewhere, immediately we're walking there. As soon as we intend to pick up something, we find our hands grasping it. Our tongue, feet, and hands work as freely as we want, and therefore we take for granted that our thoughts are the master of our body, and that this thinking is *I*.

Consequently, we try to arrange and manage everything through our thoughts. However, we find that things don't work out well, and the thinking *I* suffers in the end. Here's a familiar example: I might think I can enjoy as much of a delicious feast as I like, but if I want to digest the food quickly and smoothly, my stomach might not work as my thoughts wish. I can take some medicine or see a doctor if I want. That's possible. But when the medicine doesn't help and the doctor gives up, *I* can no longer do as *I* like, and *I* suffer.

When we consider facts like these carefully, we come to understand that our thoughts are neither the masters of our bodies nor the *I* itself. It would be more pertinent to consider our thoughts secretions of our brain, just as salivary glands secrete saliva, and the stomach secretes gastric juices. In any case, the sense of *I* produced by our minds certainly isn't the master of the whole person.

What a relief! When we realize our thoughts can't control everything, and we let go of them, the heavy meal in our stomach is digested—whether we think about it or not. Even while *I* am sleeping, I continue breathing the necessary breaths per minute. This is how the self lives.

What on earth is this *self*? I can't help but feel this is the self that is connected with the universe. In spring, buds emerge; in autumn, leaves fall. All these things including our *self* are the expression of nature's great life force.

SHOHAKU OKUMURA:

When he was young, Sawaki Roshi studied Yogacara as preparation for studying Dogen. He often uses Yogacara teachings when he points out how deeply deluded we are. His sayings in the previous chapters, 59 and 60, are examples.

However, Sawaki Roshi's teachings about zazen practice are solely based on Dogen Zenji's teachings. In chapters 61 to 65, Sawaki Roshi's expressions of "the self that is connected with the universe" are characteristic of Dogen Zenji's teachings on zazen in "Bendowa."

Rene Descartes said, "I think, therefore I am." Buddhism goes in the opposite direction. The essential teaching of Mahayana is, as the Heart Sutra says, "The five aggregates are empty." This means that *I* and its objects are productions of the five aggregates: form (in our case, body), sensation, perception, formation, and consciousness (that is, the functions of our mind). Therefore *I* does not exist independently. Not only *I* but also objects (things) are empty, meaning without fixed identity.

Because of negative-sounding expressions such as emptiness, Buddhism is sometimes considered a pessimistic or nihilistic religion. But this is only a partial understanding. Emptiness, or the lack of fixed entities existing independently of others, means we're connected with everything in the universe. This interconnectedness is called *true self*, so in fact *no self* and *true self* are the same. Sawaki Roshi's expression "the self that is connected with the universe" refers to this reality of interconnectedness.

62.

The Anxieties of Making a Living

KODO SAWAKI:
You should be embarrassed if you're unable to live without money.

KOSHO UCHIYAMA:
About ten years ago, the branch manager of one of the top banks in the center of a big city came to visit, and he revealed his agony. He said, "My retirement is getting closer, and I'm so worried about my livelihood in the years after retirement that I can't sleep at night." In spite of myself, I replied:

> You ask too much! You get a big paycheck every month and also a regular bonus. You must have savings. Look at my situation. Since I've never had a regular income, need-less to say, I have no savings. Every day I go begging like a stray dog. I've been living my life telling myself, "It will be all right if I can just make it through today." No matter how many years I continue this way of life, I will not get any bonus, retirement allowance, or pension. Your anxiety about your old age cannot be compared with mine.
>
> Your idea is to first estimate how many more years you will live, then multiply that by your salary and bonuses. You'll be able to have peace of mind only if you have the necessary amount of cash in front of you. But it's impossi-ble to feel safe that way, so you can't avoid anxiety.
>
> We may think that people who hold themselves dear,

thinking only of their own profit, saying "Me, Me, Me," will take care of themselves perfectly and live happy lives. But that's not the case. On the contrary, such people are always anxious and continuously complain that things don't go as they desire. This is a strange thing. The more they're concerned with their profit, the more they feel that things in this world never go as they wish. This fact becomes larger and larger, and they feel oppressed by things against their will. They have more and more anxieties.

On the other hand, if we can give up our self-centered concerns and see that this world doesn't exist only to satisfy our desires, then just as in begging, we cannot help but appreciate the things we receive as blessings.

After talking with him, I thought, "In this world, some people have such luxurious anxieties."

 SHOHAKU OKUMURA:
In *Pensees*, Blaise Pascal wrote:

> Man is but a reed, the most feeble thing in nature; but he is a thinking reed. The entire universe need not arm itself to crush him. A vapour, a drop of water suffices to kill him. But, if the universe were to crush him, man would still be more noble than that which killed him, because he knows that he dies and the advantage which the universe has over him; the universe knows nothing of this.
>
> All our dignity consists, then, in thought. By it we must elevate ourselves, and not by space and time which we cannot fill. Let us endeavour, then, to think well; this is the principle of morality.

In Japan, Descartes and Pascal are the best-known European philosophers. Descartes's "I think, therefore I am" and Pascal's "Man is a thinking reed" are particularly famous; they appear in high school textbooks. For these men, rational, philosophical thinking is the source of human dignity and the basis of our souls' superiority to matter.

Thinking well is the foundation of morality and the way to conquer our passions. God is the source of reason as well as the truth found through reason.

Beginning in the mid-nineteenth century, reason began to negate the existence of God. At the same time, rational thought became a tool to discover principles in nature that we could appropriate to make our lives more comfortable. Economies have developed around satisfying our desires using science and technology. As Sawaki Roshi said, schools cease being places to study truth and become factories to produce useful parts of the economic machine.

Mahayana Buddhism doesn't assume we're superior to the universe or things within it just because we have the ability to think. We ourselves are collections of the five aggregates. We can live only within the network of interconnectedness of all beings. We rely on gifts from the universe to live (air, water, food). We live together with all things. Why is it necessary to think we're superior? This is like our stomach thinking it's more valuable than other parts of our bodies.

The bank manager Uchiyama Roshi criticized is like all of us. His *I*, a fabrication of thought, is trying to put everything under its control, safe and convenient for himself as long as he lives. Because things cannot always work in accord with his desires, he experiences constant fear and frustration. This suffering arises from our narrow concept of *I*, combined with our insatiable greed.

63.

The Blessings of the Universe

KODO SAWAKI:
Heaven and earth make offerings. Air, water, plants, animals, and human beings make offerings. All things make offerings to each other. It's only within this circle of offering that we can live. Whether we appreciate this or not, it's true.

Without demanding, "Give it to me!" we make and receive offerings. The world in which we give and receive is a serene and beautiful world. It differs from the world of scrambling for things. It's vast and boundless.

KOSHO UCHIYAMA:
In Matthew 10:29, the Bible says, "Are not two sparrows sold for a penny? And not one of them falls to the ground apart from the will of your Father." Heaven and earth, all the ten thousand things, freely give us 99.99 percent of our necessities. Only 0.01 percent of the things we need are subject to our decisions whether to be greedy or not.

Air, light, water, and everything else we've received since birth, all the things that are essential to us, are given as blessings. Even without making any contribution to the universe, we've been able to live until today because of these boundless blessings.

We should make efforts to reduce our greed toward the 0.01 percent of our necessities that aren't given, and we should devote ourselves to making offerings to all beings. Only then are we able to find the vast and peaceful way of life in front of us.

KODO SAWAKI:

Make offerings to the ten directions with only one attitude: "I don't covet anything." There's no offering greater than this.

KOSHO UCHIYAMA:

Before I became a monk, I looked at the world of avarice, where people always scramble for money, and I felt suffocated by it. Fortunately, I met my teacher, Sawaki Roshi, who was a living example of not coveting anything, and I became convinced there was a way of life in which I too could live without coveting things and scrambling for money. More than anything, I'm grateful that he showed me a peaceful way of life; now I can breathe deeply, as if I were a fish returned to the water. And I also vow to be a living example of offering to the ten directions with the attitude of "I don't covet anything."

SHOHAKU OKUMURA:

In *Shobogenzo Inmo* (or "Thusness"), Dogen Zenji wrote:

> We are also the furnishings existing within the ten-direction world. How do we know that we are thus? We know that the reality is thus because our bodies and minds appear within the entire world, and yet they are not our selves. Even the body is not our personal possession; our life is moving through the passage of time, and we cannot stop it even for an instant. Where have our rosy cheeks gone? Even if we wish to find them, there is no trace. When we carefully contemplate, we understand that there are many things in the past that we can never see again. The sincere red heart does not stay either—bit by bit, it is coming and going.

Precisely because we're impermanent and without fixed, independent selves, we're connected with all beings in the universe. All beings on earth developed from single-celled life. From the time life appeared, we've been evolving based on principles of change and continuity. Even the oxygen in the air was produced by living beings. Natural resources such as soil, coal, and petroleum are legacies of numberless living beings.

Sawaki Roshi and Uchiyama Roshi emphasize the attitude of "not coveting," that is, freedom from greed. They say this is the greatest offering, or *dana*. At the beginning of *Shobogenzo Bodaisatta-Shishobo* (or "The Bodhisattva's Four Embracing Dharmas") in *The Bodhisattva's Embrace*, Dogen Zenji writes, "Giving means to be not greedy." He asks us to reflect on our deeper motivations when we give. Even when our actions appear generous, if we take a close look into our mind, we almost always find greed working. We may expect some return or covet the receiver's gratitude. We may want to think we're generous or hope others will think so. Of course on the level of social morality, it's good to do good, no matter what the motivation.

However, Buddhism is not merely a teaching of social morality. If our deeper motivation is greed, then no matter how much we give, our actions cannot be *dana paramita*, the perfection of offering. They create unwholesome karma and arrogance. Yet if we take bodhisattva vows, our whole life becomes an offering, even if we have no material possessions to give. For example, the poet Ryokan supported his life by begging and receiving offerings from many people, and his life was his offering to them. Even today, many people are inspired by his poetry and calligraphy and encouraged by his life. Sawaki Roshi offered his entire life to zazen.

Just sitting, which is good for nothing, is the ultimate posture of freedom from greed.

64.

No Other

KODO SAWAKI:
Zazen is the way we tune in to the whole universe. Samadhi is practicing each and every thing with the entire universe moment by moment.

Satori is not going to a special place that is difficult to reach, but simply being natural.

KOSHO UCHIYAMA:
Sawaki Roshi often mentioned the "self connected with the universe," or the "self of the whole universe." Hearing these words, one might think zazen inflates one's body and mind to the size of the universe. That's not what he meant. If during zazen we have such a feeling, it's a delusion or a demonic state. Buddhism never discusses the size of space. As long as you compare big and small, you have a half-baked, relative point of view. To give up your limited, egocentric thoughts is the only way to live the life that is connected with the universe, right now, right here.

For example, when we go to a public bath, the bathhouse can be the universe for us; we can try to take a bath while tuned to the whole universe. We should consider other people's feelings and avoid disturbing them. We should consider those who'll bathe after us, and keep the water clean and the area neat. We should pay attention so that everyone can enjoy the bath. This is how to take a bath connected with the entire universe.

On a train, at work, or at home with family, there's a way of being tuned to the entire universe. We should make this effort as the essence of our lives rather than discussing it as etiquette or morality.

KODO SAWAKI:
It's impossible for a fish to say, "I've swum the whole ocean," or for a bird to say, "I've flown the entire sky." But fish do swim the whole ocean, and birds do fly the entire sky. Both killifish and whales swim the whole river and ocean. This isn't a matter of quantity, but quality. We work with our bodies within only three square feet, but we work the whole heaven and earth.

Since all things are included within the self, we should conduct ourselves carefully, considering everyone's feelings.

SHOHAKU OKUMURA:
Uchiyama Roshi uses the public bath as an example of our awakening to universal self. Until about fifty years ago, the bath was a neighborhood gathering place in Japan. Most Japanese people would have understood this expression of the importance of considering others and living in harmony. These days, since most families have their own bath at home, not many people go to the public bath.

The teaching of the boundless universal self manifested in every aspect of our daily lives originated in the Zen tradition with Dogen Zenji. The community of his monastery was a universe, a miniature model of the network of interdependent origination. All people, activities, buildings, and objects in the monastery were part of this network. The training monks living in the monks' hall had no privacy at all. They practiced zazen, ate, worked, slept—they literally did everything together, twenty-four hours a day. Each person's actions influenced the whole community, like a symphony in which every musician's part is connected with everyone else's, and as a whole they make a single sound.

Dogen Zenji wrote extensively about this aspect of monastic practice. Six important writings were later compiled as *Eihei Shingi*, or *Dogen's Pure Standards*. In one of these, "Tenzokyokun" or "Instructions for the Cook," he wrote, "From the beginning in Buddha's family there have been six temple administrators. They are all Buddha's children and together they carry out Buddha's work."

Not only people sitting in the monks' hall, but also those working in the kitchen and other departments carry out Buddha's work. What is Buddha's work? To awaken and manifest the true reality of all things, known by these expressions: impermanence, no self, emptiness, interdependent origination.

For a tenzo, a cook, Buddha's work is devoting his or her life right now, right here, to preparing meals for the community. To do this, the tenzo needs to work in harmony with all things and people in the kitchen. Dogen wrote, "When you take care of things, do not see with your common eyes, do not think with your common sentiments. Pick a single blade of grass and erect a sanctuary for the jewel king; enter a single atom and turn the great wheel of the teaching." This "great wheel of the teaching" refers to the Buddha's Dharma wheel. The tenzo expounds the Buddha's teachings through his or her work.

Sawaki Roshi's comment about fish and birds comes from Dogen Zenji's Genjokoan. By wholeheartedly swimming or flying their corners of ocean or sky, fish and birds live the entire universe.

65

True Self Beyond Thinking

KODO SAWAKI:
The true self is not the *I* that is the product of my individual thought. That's it!

KOSHO UCHIYAMA:
In the *Analects* Confucius said, "I don't want to say anything. . . . What does heaven say? The four seasons keep coming around, and the hundred things keep arising. But what does heaven say?" This doesn't sound like Confucius. But when I think of this saying as a reflection of the state of mind he reached in his later years after having done so much, it doesn't seem strange to me.

In Ryokan's poem:

As my keepsake
What can I leave?
In spring, flowers.
In summer, cuckoos.
And in fall, maple leaves.

If you look at the words of Confucius and Ryokan in light of Sawaki Roshi's expression "The true self is not the *I* that is the product of my individual thought," you might come to understand what they mean.

Precisely because the self that is not the product of thought is beyond thinking, we cannot define it. However, I think we can understand that our true self is not limited by the scope of our thoughts. The true self lies beyond such boundaries. It's the self that is connected with the universe. It's "the four seasons come around" and "in spring, flowers. In summer, cuckoos. And in fall, maple leaves." This self is not the *I* that is jealous of others' happiness and glad at their sadness, thinking, "Thankfully that didn't happen to me." Rather, our true self rejoices over others' happiness from the bottom of our hearts and truly shares their sorrows.

KODO SAWAKI:
The root source of delusions takes place when we begin to think *I.*

Many people complain, "I'm busy, busy!" What are they so busy with? They're busy being used by their delusory desires. That's all.

The true reality of all things is resolved, at peace. There's no need to try to twist things into what we want.

SHOHAKU OKUMURA:
Confucius tried to teach kings and ministers to govern with principles and benevolence, but his attempts were not completely successful. Although his teachings were appreciated and became the central philosophy of China, his life, particularly in later years, had many hardships, and he was disappointed in the conditions of Chinese society.

That's why Uchiyama Roshi thinks this saying about the silence of heaven came from his final days. Many things happen in each season, yet heaven says nothing; therefore Confucius didn't want to say anything. From this, Uchiyama Roshi supposes that in Confucius' final days, he didn't have much hope of improving society through human effort, so he felt it was better to leave everything to the natural movement of heaven.

Ryokan's poem is based on Dogen Zenji's poem "Original Face." In Steven Heine's translation:

In spring, the cherry blossoms,
In summer, the cuckoo's song,
In autumn, the moon, shining,
In winter, the frozen snow:
How pure and clear are the seasons!

The things that make the seasons beautiful throughout the year are the original face of ourselves. Uchiyama Roshi often said that the life force that enables us to breathe a certain number of times a minute even while we sleep is the same as the power that makes the autumn leaves turn red.

Because he had so few personal possessions, Ryokan said his keepsake to offer was everything in nature. His poems and his life without greed and self-centeredness were his offerings.

Sawaki Roshi's "homeless" life without a temple was the same. While alive, he used his veteran's pension to print the texts he lectured on, which he gave to practitioners. When he died, his body was donated to the Kyoto University hospital, his books to the Komazawa University library. In the end, his zazen practice with thousands of people was his offering and legacy. Within our zazen, he still lives.

66.

Enriching Our Lives

KODO SAWAKI:
No matter how much you suffer in the transitory world, you cannot enrich your life. But when you embrace the transient world as the content of zazen, your practice of Buddhadharma and your life will be enriched.

KOSHO UCHIYAMA:
A woman once said to me, "You know a lot about the world even though you stay in your temple and practice zazen most of the time." I don't think what she said is true. There can't be many people my age this ignorant of the world. I've had a regular salary for only six months out of sixty years. The rest of the time, I haven't been involved in the life of the usual world; instead I've spent my time doing zazen, begging, cleaning the temple, weeding the garden, cutting firewood, cooking, and so on. I read the newspaper but have no radio or TV. I don't have much information about what goes on in society.

However, some people come to me for advice or visit and say they're impressed with my writings. It seems that in some ways I know more about human life than people in the world. In the ordinary world people experience so much excitement and receive so much information every day that they become paralyzed and lose the critical eyes to see the connections among events.

For example, if we often see violent government debates on TV, our senses become numb, and we just take for granted that the government is such a place. However, if we lead a life of zazen in a temple without TV, and we happen to glimpse such a scene, we're shocked. We come to understand that this world is an absurd place when we see that even in national politics, important decisions are made with the same sordid violence we see in gang fights.

If we live amid noise, we cease to notice it. If we're in a quiet place, leading a life of zazen, we can see the true face of the world.

KODO SAWAKI:
Unless you see the "human" from Buddha's point of view, you'll never understand the truth.

SHOHAKU OKUMURA:
Sawaki Roshi's expression "embrace the transient world as the content of zazen" means seeing objectively and critically, free from our narrowly self-centered perspective. Usually we evaluate things only in terms of benefit to ourselves. If we practice perceiving events as combinations of causes and conditions, then we're practicing seeing from Buddha's point of view.

In the second decade of the twenty-first century, we have much more information from around the world than Uchiyama Roshi had in the 1960s. As a result, we experience not only numbness but also fear for the future of human civilization.

What makes a rich life? Have our lives been enriched by the mass of information we receive day after day through the media? I don't think so. Our lives have become more and more busy and convenient but not necessarily richer. However, I don't think if we merely sit silently in a temple, we enrich our lives.

Uchiyama Roshi often said that when he met visitors who asked his advice, he met them as part of his own life, embracing their problems as his own. If he needed information, he read books and consulted people. Even though he wasn't involved directly in the mundane world, he was always curious about what was happening and why.

For example, he was particularly interested in and worried about the condition of Japanese education. He contributed a series of articles to a magazine for schoolteachers. Later these were published as a book entitled *Education: Growing Together*. Because teachers enrich their lives through their work, they and their students grow together.

Uchiyama Roshi was financially poor and lived quietly, but he welcomed people and sincerely met and listened to them. This enabled him to live an exceptionally rich life.

67.

Live Your Own Life

KODO SAWAKI:
As far as you can see, there's only you and nothing else. "I feel blah . . . keep me company," you might say, "take over my pain." You wish!

KOSHO UCHIYAMA:
Recently a man enticed several young women to take a drive with him, then beat and killed them. Why did he do this?

According to the newspaper, he had been in prison. Released after serving his sentence, he found his wife had left him, and he was cast out of society. It seems the motive for his crimes was revenge. He turned his back on the world and showed people how evil a man rejected by his family and society could become. He decided to be as vicious as possible.

I don't know what kind of circumstances he grew up in, but this kind of attitude can often be seen in overprotected children. Such children never learn to control their desires. As adults, they can't put on the brakes, and so naturally they crash. Because their parents always clean up after their mistakes, they grow up without ever learning that only we ourselves live our lives. This is the most important lesson.

When spoiled children, perhaps now adults, fall into some terrible predicament from which their parents are unable to extricate them, they think, "All right then. I'll try to be as bad as possible. When I'm executed, my parents will be sorry, and other people will be frightened." Acting in defiance of their parents and society, they ruin the most precious thing: their own lives.

Such overprotected children are unable to arrive at a true self or the determination "I will live my own life." When they experience difficulties, they can't endure their troubles and lack the resilience to recover. It's not possible to live our lives without mistakes and problems. I hope we understand that we need to be patient when we encounter trying situations and trust that we have the life energy we need to regain our footing. I repeat: We have to live out our lives by ourselves.

SHOHAKU OKUMURA:

"Overprotected children" is an expression that emerged in Japan around 1970. It's similar to the American phrase "helicopter parenting."

Before World War II, people had large families; the Japanese government encouraged this to support a strong empire. For example, my mother had seven siblings. After the war, families had fewer children: only one or two. Parents became overly protective of their children. They tried to shield them from any difficulty and allowed them to do whatever they wanted. Such parents failed to make their children independent enough to mature. Some children didn't learn to sympathize with others. Some didn't know how to control their desires, so they did wrong things and destroyed their lives. When Uchiyama Roshi read the newspaper article, he thought this criminal might be an extreme example of such a person.

Uchiyama Roshi admitted he himself was an early example of an overprotected child. He came from a wealthy family, and everything he wanted was provided. But after he became a monk, he couldn't rely on anyone. He had to do everything by himself. He felt that the hardships experienced by overprotected children trying to become independent were worse than those suffered by children raised without much support. In this respect, Sawaki Roshi and Uchiyama Roshi were opposites. In Sawaki Roshi's childhood, he had no protection at all.

In a sense, Shakyamuni Buddha was an earlier example of an overprotected child. His father, King Suddhodana, provided all the luxuries to satisfy him and tried to hide anything negative from his son. When Shakyamuni was almost grown and went outside the palace, he was surprised to see the suffering of old age, sickness, and death.

According to Maurice Walshe's translation of *Digha Nikaya*, at the end of his final summer practice period, shortly before his death, the Buddha said, "You should live as islands unto yourselves, being your own refuge, with no one else as your refuge, with the Dhamma as an island, with the Dhamma as your refuge, with no other refuge."

68

A Burglar Breaks into an Empty House

KODO SAWAKI:
Once a monk asked Master Longya, "How did the ancient master finally cease doing things and completely settle down?"

Longya replied, "It was like a thief slipping into a vacant house."

A burglar breaks into an empty house. He can't steal anything. There's no need to escape. Nobody chases him. It's nothing. Understand: It's nothing.

Satori is like a burglar breaking into an empty house. Although he had difficulty getting in, there's nothing to steal. He doesn't need to run. Nobody's after him. The whole thing is a flop.

KOSHO UCHIYAMA:
Sawaki Roshi often spoke of a burglar breaking into an empty house. Someone who happened to hear this wrote that Sawaki Roshi had said, "When you do zazen, you shouldn't do it like a burglar breaking into an empty house, because there's no gain in that." When I read this, I was amazed. What an unbelievable misunderstanding. If Sawaki Roshi were alive, I can't imagine how he would react!

Discussing Buddhist teachings is totally different from ordinary discussion, which is based on common sense. We must listen carefully to a teacher and read texts with a calm mind; I recommend not trying to understand them on your own.

This "burglar breaking into an empty house" is Sawaki Roshi's translation of Longya's saying, "It was like a crook slipping into a vacant house." This is the answer to the question, "How do we finally settle down?" or "Where's the true refuge in our lives?" After all his efforts, the thief gets into a vacant house. There's nothing to steal, nobody to flee from. There's nothing but the self that is only the self in the empty house. At this point, there's nothing to give or take, and there's no relation to others. We might feel such a life is not worth living. But satori, the final place to settle down in one's life, is to take this basic attitude: "That which lives out my life is nothing other than myself." Satori is simply settling down here and now, where things are unsatisfactory.

SHOHAKU OKUMURA:

Longya Judun (835–923), known in Japanese as Ryuge Koton, was a disciple of Dongshan Liangjie (807–69). Known in Japanese as Tozan Ryokai, Dongshan was the founder of the Caodong school, the Chinese school that Dogen Zenji studied before he founded the Soto school in Japan. The ancient master in the monk's question refers to Shishuang Qingzhu (807–88), or Sekiso Keisho in Japanese. Shishuang was Dongshan's Dharma cousin.

In case 96 of the *Book of Serenity*, Shishuang said, "Cease doing. Stop the separation between subject and object. Be like one moment is ten thousand years. Be like cold ashes and dead trees. Be like a strip of white silk." To be like cold ashes and dead trees is to be without discrimination; to be like a strip of white silk is to be without defilement.

The koan continues. After Shishuang's death, his attendant asked the head monk the meaning of this saying. The monk replied, "It clarifies the matter of absolute oneness." The attendant didn't agree. Then the head monk died in zazen. The attendant patted his back and said, "You don't understand the late teacher's meaning even in a dream."

Later a monk asked Longya about the meaning of Shishuang's "cease doing." Longya said, "It's like a crook slipping into a vacant house." This saying shows Longya's understanding is very different from the head monk's. He understands ceasing as relinquishing the struggle for gain based on our desires and settling down here and now. For the head monk, ceasing is equivalent to death. This is a common misunderstanding of the Buddhist teaching of emptiness.

But as Sawaki Roshi and Uchiyama Roshi have said, our zazen is not a negation of life; it's simply stilling ourselves in the here and now without chasing satisfaction. According to Uchiyama Roshi, this is the attitude of living out our lives by ourselves, without relying on others or any particular dogma.

The Japanese haiku poet Masaoka Shiki (1867–1902) died of tuberculosis at thirty-five. In his final days he suffered unbearable pain caused by spinal decay. He couldn't even shift in his bed. About three months before his death, he wrote in an essay for a newspaper: "Until now, I have misunderstood satori in Zen. I mistakenly thought that satori was to die with peace of mind in any condition. Satori is to live with peace of mind in any condition."

I think this is the difference between the understanding of the head monk and Longya. In *Shobogenzo Shoji* (or "Life and Death"), Dogen said, "Just understand that life and death is itself nirvana and neither dislike life and death nor seek after nirvana. Only then will it be possible for us to be released from life and death. . . . This present life and death is the life of Buddha."

69

Thief's Action and Buddha's Action

KODO SAWAKI:

Once someone asked me, "I understand that when we do zazen, we manifest buddha, but when we don't do zazen, are we just ordinary deluded people?" Do you think that when you're stealing something, you're a thief, but when you aren't stealing, you aren't a thief? You can eat rice to commit a robbery or to practice zazen. Is it the same or different? Even if a person steals only once, he's a thief; even though we do zazen for only one period, we do zazen forever.

How could it be that only Ishikawa Goemon is a thief and one who steals on the spur of the moment isn't? Anyone who steals on impulse is surely a crook. In the same way, not only is Shakyamuni a buddha, but anyone who does zazen following the Buddha is a buddha.

KOSHO UCHIYAMA:

When he talked about the Buddha's action of zazen, Sawaki Roshi often referred to "thief's action" as a way to get through to people. I'd like to look at his explanation of a thief's action and a buddha's action. This is also a comparison between the secular and religious views of these actions.

Even though we might have more or less a buddha's view and character, if we steal on impulse, imitating Ishikawa Goemon, then in both worldly and religious views, we've forever committed a thief's deed. The world takes legal action against our crime and treats us coldly and suspiciously for the rest of our lives.

On the other hand, from the religious perspective, that's not the end of the story. Even though we have the flaw of our crime, if we perform a buddha's action, following Shakyamuni, what's the result? Though we have more or less a criminal's outlook and character, our buddha's action causes our everlasting redemption. To act, whether as a thief or a buddha, is to manifest everlasting thief or everlasting buddha here in this moment. Therefore, there's a gate to redemption even for a condemned prisoner.

What's the basic difference between the secular and religious worlds? In the secular world, other people judge and evaluate a person. In the religious world, there's no such relationship. This is the world of "the reality of the self" and "the self that is only the self."

In the world in which we judge, we evaluate a person and easily conclude that they're superior or inferior, good or bad. We fix this evaluation and brand the person. However, this fixed evaluation has nothing to do with the reality of that person. The truth of life cannot be so simple.

No one can be a thief from head to toe, and no one can be a buddha from head to toe. In the religious world, no matter how badly we've behaved, it's possible to be redeemed from our misdeeds if we repent them and return to our true and ever fresh self. On the other hand, even someone as great as a buddha cannot accumulate and preserve good deeds for the future—he or she cannot be fixed as a buddha.

Therefore, if we take a crook's action right now, the entirety of our self at this moment becomes an everlasting crook. If we take a buddha's action right now, our whole self becomes an everlasting buddha. Regardless of what we did before, in each moment we should aim at a buddha's action right now, right here. This and only this is the true aim for human beings.

KODO SAWAKI:
Zazen is not something we can store up. Shinran rejected the idea of saving up nembutsu. In Shin Buddhism it's said that storing up practice is done by self-power mentality.

Imagine someone saying, "Since I was young, I've been very honest. So lately I've stopped being honest and occasionally steal." We can't hoard credit for our good deeds.

Like Ishikawa Goemon, the moment we steal, we enter the thief realm. Like Buddha, when we do zazen, we immediately enter the tathagata realm.

SHOHAKU OKUMURA:

At the end of *Shobogenzo Hotsubodaishin* (or "Arousing Bodhi-Mind"), Dogen Zenji quotes Nagarjuna's definition of a demon. Nagarjuna said there are four kinds of demon, but they're all simply the five aggregates: "The demon of the five aggregates refers to the causes and conditions that combine to produce delusive desires."

On the other hand, Dogen Zenji wrote in *Shobogenzo Makahan-nyaharamitsu* (or Maha-prajna-paramita, Perfection of Great Wisdom), "The time of Avalokiteshvara Bodhisattva practicing profound prajna paramita is the whole body clearly seeing the emptiness of all five aggregates. The five aggregates are forms, sensations, perceptions, formations, and consciousness; this is the fivefold prajna."

The five aggregates, our body and mind, can be a demon that produces delusive desires—or a wisdom that frees us from them. What enables this transformation of body and mind from demon to wisdom? When Sawaki Roshi talks about thief's action and buddha's action, he's referring to this transformation. We have both thief nature and buddha nature. But unless we actually steal, we're not a thief; unless we practice Buddha's way, we're not a buddha. Our action in each moment manifests everlasting thief or buddha nature.

This teaching comes from Dogen's expression *gyobutsu*, or Practice Buddha. In *Shobogenzo Gyobutsu-igi*, he interprets the expression *gyo-butsuigi*, which means practicing Buddha's dignified conduct, as *gyobutsu-igi*, or dignified conduct of Practice Buddha. He presents a buddha whose name is Action or Practice.

When we practice a buddha's action, our practice is buddha. It's not that we as karmic individuals become enlightened buddhas for the rest of our lives. In each moment we practice and manifest buddha. This is also the meaning of what Dogen Zenji said in *Shobogenzo Genjokoan*: "When buddhas are truly buddhas, they don't need to perceive they are buddhas; however, they are enlightened buddhas, and they continue actualizing buddha."

70

The "What Am I Going to Do?" Dance

KODO SAWAKI:
I once saw a play with a character who wondered, "What am I going to do? What am I going to do? Oh! What am I going to do?" I've never had such bad fortune that I had to ask, "What am I going to do?" because I see that nothing is worth worrying about.

KOSHO UCHIYAMA:
This world is like a muddy pond where everyone is squirming like a mosquito larva crying, "What am I going to do?" The root of this "What am I going to do?" dance is karma. Karma is any action we take with the desire for satisfaction. We always take action based on our desires. When things turn out as we want, we give a big smile. Whenever things don't happen as we expect, we spin in circles, saying, "Oh! What am I going to do?"

But in fact, good and bad luck, happiness and unhappiness, right and wrong in this world are not the way we see, hear, and think of them from the viewpoint of our personal desires. If we understand this, we can't help but begin to doubt the narrow framework of our thoughts. And by questioning our own assumptions, we come to understand that while we should make an effort, there's no need to try desperately to control everything. When we realize this, the fretting mind magically disappears.

Suffering arises as a reaction to the frustration of desire, so whenever we act according to desire, anguish eventually materializes in front of us like a cloud.

KODO SAWAKI:

Amitabha Buddha says, "Don't worry, no sentient being is forever lost in delusion. You're okay. Relax!" Still, sentient beings are always wailing, "Oh, no! This is terrible!"

Happiness or unhappiness, superiority or inferiority, like or dislike, good or bad—in this world, people are in an uproar about them. The world in which nothing is worth worrying about is beyond thinking. In this world, we remove the framework of human thoughts by just sitting.

SHOHAKU OKUMURA:

In the 1970s I practiced at a small zendo in western Massachusetts with two Dharma brothers from Antaiji. We supported our practice with odd jobs, including working as janitors at a tofu factory.

At the time, I didn't have a driver's license. Leaving the zendo after lunch, I walked an hour to the nearest town and then hitchhiked about twenty miles to a larger town, where the factory was. I worked from 4 to 10 p.m. and slept on a pile of soybean bags in the factory. The next morning, I hitchhiked back and returned to the zendo a little before noon. It took me almost twenty-four hours to work for six hours.

One winter day, I woke at the factory in the morning and started to walk toward the edge of town where I could hitchhike. Everything was covered in snow, and it was quite cold. I wasn't particularly depressed, but I was tired. I thought, "What am I doing here? Why do I have to do such a silly thing—be a janitor at a tofu factory in the U.S.? I came from Japan to establish a place to share Zen Buddhist practice. Only a few Americans even know we're here. This is not only hard; it's ridiculous. It might be better to go back to Japan to continue this practice. Or I might go to a big city and practice at a large Zen center with more Americans."

Another part of myself counterargued, "This isn't foolish at all. What I'm doing is not just being a janitor at a factory to make a little money. I'm part of the stream of Buddhism coming to the West. Everything I'm doing is for the sake of the Dharma. In ancient times, many Buddhist monks suffered greater hardships. If I can't make it through this, then wherever I go, I'll have the same problem. Stop complaining and just do it."

Walking on the snowy street, I was arguing back and forth with myself. When I arrived at the intersection where I could hitchhike, I went into a shop and ordered coffee and a doughnut. An elderly waitress brought them to me and said, "Smile! It's a beautiful day." I guess my face wasn't cheerful.

I looked out the window. There was a beautiful blue sky. I hadn't noticed it while I was walking and thinking. I realized nothing was lacking at that moment—a cup of hot coffee and a doughnut in a warm coffee shop under a beautiful sky were all I needed.

Even today I appreciate the offering of kind speech from the old waitress. Her encouraging words helped me stop the "What am I going to do?" dance and return to here and now. Since then, whenever I enter a labyrinth of thought, I remember her saying, "Smile! It's a beautiful day."

71.

Aiming in Emptiness

KODO SAWAKI:
Fundamentally we can walk in any direction: east, west, south, or north—whichever way we wish.

Each and every activity permeates the entire ten-direction world. We simply practice manifesting eternity through our action in each moment.

Once Sen no Rikyu needed a carpenter to drive a nail into an ornamental alcove post in a teahouse. After looking here and there, Rikyu decided on the best spot. The carpenter marked it—and then took a break. Afterward, he couldn't find the tiny mark. He asked Rikyu to search again for the best location. After a while, the tea master decided on the spot and indicated to the carpenter, "Right there!" When the carpenter looked carefully, he found it was the very place he had marked the first time.

Don't you see? There's always clear aim right in the midst of emptiness in which nothing is fixed. We must have a decisive direction.

KOSHO UCHIYAMA:
East, west, south, or north, whichever way we go, we just live the self that is only the self, and fortunately there's no direction forbidden us. So it's okay for us to stride majestically wherever we go as the self that is only the self, with peace of mind. But at the same time, in the midst of formlessness, which demands no particular direction, there must be a decisive aim. No matter what we do, we should do it so each of our actions expands throughout the entire ten-direction world. Eternity is manifested in each moment.

Because I live a lax and unsophisticated life, I would simply drive a nail into the post in a haphazard way, without asking a carpenter. But for someone like Sen no Rikyu, who sees into emptiness, there must be a way of driving a nail as an expression of formlessness. We human beings may stride in any direction: east, west, south, or north—whichever way we like. Only when we actualize the self that permeates the entire ten-direction world and practice manifesting eternity moment by moment will the peace of the self that is only the self no matter what ripen.

KODO SAWAKI:

The truth of Buddhism is realized only through practice; it is attained through the body. The way we use our muscles must be in accordance with zazen. Practicing zazen, we train our attitude toward life in each and every activity. This is practice. Within it, we actualize true peace of mind.

SHOHAKU OKUMURA:

Sen no Rikyu (1522–91) was the founder of the Senke school of tea ceremony. His style, called *wabi-cha*, emphasizes simplicity and serenity. He conducted the tea ceremony in a very small grass-thatched teahouse, which allowed host and guest to be in true intimacy. He made this ceremony a spiritual path. He also practiced Rinzai Zen at Nanshuji in Sakai, his hometown, and at Daitokuji in Kyoto. His lineage practices the oneness of tea and Zen.

Since a teahouse is small and simple, it's important to locate everything in its proper place. In this story, Rikyu has a carpenter driving a nail into an alcove post, probably to hang a flower vase. The flowers and scroll on the alcove wall were the only decorations. It must have been important for his sense of aesthetics to find the best places for them.

Aiming refers to our actions for achieving a certain goal through thinking based on conventional truth. *Formlessness* refers to ultimate truth, oneness, equality, eternity, and freedom. Everything we see has form, which is why we have perception. Formlessness emphasizes that these things don't exist the way we see them. The Diamond Sutra says, "To see all forms as no form is to see the Tathataga." Later, this truth, this reality of no form, was given the philosophical expression *emptiness*. This interpenetration of conventional and ultimate truth is the foundation of Zen teaching.

There's a story in *Dogen's Pure Standards* about Shishuang Qingzhu, who appeared in chapter 68. When he was young and still training, Shishuang became rice manager in the great Zen master Guishan's assembly. One day Shishuang was in the storehouse sifting rice.

> Guishan said, "Food from donors should not be scattered around."
>
> Shishuang said, "It's not scattered around."
>
> Guishan picked up one grain from the floor and said, "You say it's not scattered around, but where does this come from?"
>
> Shishuang did not reply.
>
> Guishan again said, "Do not disdain even this single grain. A hundred thousand grains can be born from this single grain."
>
> Shishuang said, "A hundred thousand grains can be born from this single grain. But it's not yet clear; where did this single grain come from?"
>
> Guishan laughed loudly, "Ho! Ho!" and returned to the abbot's quarters. Later in the evening he went up to lecture in the hall and said, "Oh Great Assembly, there's a worm in the rice."

Guishan cautions his rice manager that he shouldn't waste even one grain, a precious offering from donors that has the potential to produce a hundred thousand grains if planted. The young monk points out the emptiness of all things; nothing is coming and going, even a grain of rice. There's no discrimination between waste and not-waste. Why is it waste if the grain doesn't go through a human body? A scattered grain of rice can be eaten by a bird. Is it wasted? Whether it goes through a human's or bird's body, the grain is simply part of the circulation within the network of interdependent origination. It's waste only from a human point of view.

In each and every action we need to have a precise and concrete aim that expresses emptiness.

72

Sawaki Roshi's Last Words

KODO SAWAKI:
It's pointless for human beings merely to live a life that lasts seventy or eighty years.

KOSHO UCHIYAMA:
Sawaki Roshi traveled alone to teach all over Japan until he was eighty-three, but when his legs became weak, he retired to Antaiji. In the afternoons, I served tea in his room. One day he admonished me with the saying above. At the time, I simply agreed, and our conversation moved to other topics. Looking back, I regret that I didn't hear more teachings on this point.

Now I've retired from Antaiji. I begin to think that dying is the only practice remaining to me; I have to straightforwardly face and tackle the matter of my own life and death. In this situation, I remember these words of Sawaki Roshi and think this must be the most important saying he left me—his final teaching.

KODO SAWAKI:
It's very unskillful to use this body of five feet only as a five-foot body. It's foolish to live merely using up fifty, eighty, or one hundred years of longevity. To practice the buddha way is to become a person who will never die, who is not at all different from the buddha pervading the entire universe forever.

KOSHO UCHIYAMA:
Sawaki Roshi passed away on December 21, 1965. When he was dying he was peaceful. He didn't leave any dying verse or will. I still

clearly remember how he was all that day, from morning until his death. His death was calm and natural, like a tree falling. That's the only way I can describe it.

He sometimes said, "When I die, call the Kyoto University hospital, and donate my body to them. After that, you can just drink sake. It's no use clumsily chanting sutras with your sad voices." I donated his body to the hospital and could think of no other way to express my gratitude to my teacher besides doing a forty-nine-day sesshin as his funeral. I completed that.

I've been able to live until today without many troubles because whenever I have difficulty, I remember my teacher's words, which live deep in my mind, and follow his teachings. His sayings are his legacy.

SHOHAKU OKUMURA:
This final chapter was added by Shusoku Kushiya, Uchiyama Roshi's disciple and the editor of the 2006 Japanese version of this book. Originally this was part of an essay by Uchiyama Roshi that appeared in the August 1985 issue of the Buddhist magazine *Daihorin*. Uchiyama Roshi was then seventy-three.

As in chapter 71, Uchiyama Roshi and Sawaki Roshi are discussing finding eternity in each moment.

According to the Buddhist Text Translation Society's rendering of the Sutra of Buddha's Last Teaching (or Butsu-yuikyo-gyo), right before passing away, Shakyamuni said, "From now on all of my disciples must continuously practice. Then the Thus Come One's Dharma body will always be present and indestructible."

When we practice buddha's action like a burglar breaking into an empty house, letting go of self-centered, hunting mind, each moment manifests the eternal Dharma body of the tathagata. This is what Sawaki Roshi means when he says it's pointless to live a life that lasts only seventy or eighty years. Our five aggregates last as an individual at most several decades and then disperse. When we drop off body and mind as Mara and express prajna, or wisdom, then our impermanent, conditioned bodies and minds manifest the eternal Dharma body. Living this way is becoming a person who will never die.

About the same time Uchiyama Roshi wrote this article, he also wrote a collection of poems on life and death. The last poem, which I also mentioned in chapter 29, is as follows:

SAMADHI OF THE TREASURY OF THE
RADIANT LIGHT

Though poor, never poor
Though sick, never sick
Though aging, never aging
Though dying, never dying
Reality prior to division—
Herein lies unlimited depth

Uchiyama Roshi passed away on March 13, 1998, at Nokein, Uji. He was eighty-five years old. That was the fifteenth day of the second month in the lunar calendar, Shakyamuni Buddha's Parinirvana Day. The temple was illuminated by bright moonlight. Uchiyama Roshi died as if sleeping peacefully.

I've been studying and practicing following Dogen Zenji's teachings since I was nineteen. Dogen Zenji and his teachings have been like a great mountain for me. I've been trying to climb, but the mountain is steep and high. After more than forty years, I feel I'm still a beginner. However, my aging body has already passed Dogen Zenji's; he died when he was fifty-three. Thus, Sawaki Roshi's and Uchiyama Roshi's teachings and examples of practicing with aging bodies and minds in the final stage of human life have been precious to me.

Kodo Sawaki Roshi's Zazen
by Kosho Uchiyama

What Buddhadharma Is, What Zazen Is, and How We Can Live Based on Them

This essay is based on Uchiyama Roshi's 1980 talk at Jinnoin temple in Hiroshima Prefecture—one of the temples Sawaki Roshi visited regularly as a part of his "moving monastery."

To me the temple Jinnoin is strongly associated with the memory of my late teacher, Kodo Sawaki Roshi. He regularly visited here. On his last trip he lectured on the theme "Others Are Not Me." His talk was noted in shorthand by a reporter from the *Asahi Shimbun* and appeared in the religious section of that newspaper.

After this visit, Sawaki Roshi returned to Tokyo and prepared for a trip to the Tohoku region. He arrived at his first destination, Ofunato, but found he was unable to continue traveling. He returned to Tokyo and sent me a telegram reading, "Come and pick me up." I hurried there and took him to Kyoto. From then on, he stayed in Kyoto, spending his final days at Antaiji. In my mind, Jinnoin is the place Sawaki Roshi gave his final Dharma talk. That was in the late spring of 1963. Whenever I visit Jinnoin, I reminisce about Sawaki Roshi with the abbot and his wife.

I first listened to a Dharma talk by Sawaki Roshi during the summer zazen gathering at Sojiji in Yokohama in July 1941. I was very impressed and immediately made up my mind to become his disciple. He instructed me to go to Daichuji in Tochigi Prefecture. I entered Daichuji in August and was ordained on December 8, 1941. That was Pearl Harbor Day, when World War II began for Japan.

I had begun my practice of the buddha way a little differently from most Buddhist priests in Japan. In the English textbook I studied in middle school, I found a proverb: "Don't live to eat, but eat to live." This was only an example of how to use an English infinitive, but I was profoundly impressed by it. Reading that sentence was the starting point of my journey in search of the way.

I'm almost seventy now, and so far I have never lived to eat—this proves how strong my impression of that proverb was. I often told the Americans practicing at Antaiji that I had never worked to earn money or pursued a livelihood. Even the hippies were surprised by this. The only job I had was six months as a teacher at a Christian seminary. My salary was eighty yen a month. Altogether I earned four hundred and eighty yen. That was the only regular income I ever received.

Nowadays people say everyone should earn a living. I think this is pointless. I've always thought it enough if I can get through a day without starving. I've lived nearly seventy years this way. I know it's possible.

During World War II, however, a person with this attitude, a person who wasn't working to support the war, was shunned, and I had a very difficult time. Eventually I became malnourished and was in bed at my parents' home for two months. But I still didn't work to eat. The saying "Don't live to eat, but eat to live" has clearly influenced my life since the beginning of middle school.

By the time I was fourteen or fifteen, my thinking had become focused on the question "What is the meaning of life?" I became completely absorbed in this, always asking, "What is life? What is life?" Studying for university entrance exams wasn't important to me at all, but I asked this question of everyone who seemed capable of thinking about it.

Nearly all of them said, "I don't know about that," or "You're a strange boy, aren't you?" Occasionally someone complacently gave me a speech, but their ideas were only about how to live comfortably or climb the social ladder. No one could give me a satisfactory answer.

While searching for the answer to this question, I often visited the Holiness Church in Kanda Surugadai, close to where I lived in Hongo Motomachi, Tokyo. I learned that Christianity begins with God: God created human beings. Human beings fall into sin against God.

Through Jesus Christ, we are saved. God is the foundation and first cause of everything.

I listened to lectures on Buddhism too. The Tokyo University Young Buddhists' Association Hall held public lectures by famous scholars every Saturday. According to them, Buddhists seek awakening and nirvana. The basic premise was that Buddhism is a teaching that has "becoming a buddha" as its goal. For me, my own life was the problem. I couldn't follow those talks on God and Buddha because they didn't have anything to do with my life.

Although there weren't many new religions in those days, I did look into a few, such as Tenrikyo, Omotokyo, and so on. I was disappointed by them because they only talked about the worldly benefits gained if one believed. They too had nothing to do with my life.

From these experiences I became convinced that most Japanese never think about the question of the self and never ask themselves about the nature of life based on the self.

In ancient times, when Confucianism was introduced, Japanese people thought the benevolence and justice it emphasized were the supreme way. They simply followed what was taught. Later, when Buddhism was transmitted, they followed it and sought nirvana. I can't help thinking this is like a young man who can't find a suitable bride. When forced to marry a woman his parents find for him, he cherishes the illusion that she was his own choice and is the best possible mate. Japanese people seem to worship whatever is handed to them, instead of pursuing a life of their own.

These days, I lecture on Dogen's *Shobogenzo* monthly in Kyoto. Dogen Zenji often used the term *Buddhadharma*. Amazingly, few commentaries on *Shobogenzo* discuss the meaning of Buddhadharma. Generally, when the monks and scholars who comment on Dogen Zenji's writings encounter this term, they approach it with blind reverence, as an object of worship. They never try to figure out what it means. Japanese people don't see things through their own eyes. They don't start with the self.

In the past, religions were geographically limited. There was Christianity in the West, Buddhism in the East, and Hinduism and Islam between. Today, besides these established religions, there are countless new movements appearing in waves. These have come about because religion can be a very lucrative business. Now that the world is becoming one society, it's as if someone hit a beehive or turned over a toy box—religions are scattered everywhere. In this age, we have no yardstick to measure what true religion is.

Selecting a religion is like choosing produce in a supermarket. We walk around checking out options, shopping for a god after figuring out what we can afford. As a middle school student I was smart enough to realize that a god we shop for cannot be a genuine one, and the only thing I could do was live out the truth of my own life.

That was when I was sixteen or seventeen. However, at that time I didn't understand at all what the truth of my own life was. Since then, for about fifty years, I've been pursuing the truth of the self.

There's a well-known phrase in *Shobogenzo Genjokoan*: "To study the buddha way is to study the self." When I first encountered these words, I saw that I wasn't the only person who tried to live my own life starting from the self; I found that Dogen Zenji had the same attitude. Shakyamuni Buddha left his father's palace and devoted his life to practice because he was troubled by the suffering of human life; he had to find his own way to liberation. I understood that, but I couldn't make up my mind to shave my head and become a Buddhist monk.

About ten years later, I read *Shobogenzo Jishozanmai* (or "Samadhi of Self-Verification"), where Dogen Zenji writes:

> When we follow a teacher or a sutra to study the Dharma, we follow the self. The sutras are by nature sutras of the self. The teacher is by nature the teacher of the self. Therefore, to visit teachers widely is to visit the self widely. . . . To hold a hundred grasses is to hold the self. To hold ten thousand trees is to hold the self. We must study that the self is living through nothing other than such efforts. Within this practice we drop off the self and truly encounter and verify the self.

This means that when we practice with a teacher or study sutras, we're simply following the self. When we study a sutra, that sutra is nothing other than my own self. When we practice with a teacher, the teacher is my self. Ancient practitioners traveled to visit teachers, wearing bamboo hats, black robes, leggings, and straw sandals. They traveled without stopping until they found a true teacher. Seeking a teacher in this way is nothing other than seeking one's own self.

In holding whatever you encounter, you simply hold the self. We live by experiencing all things. All things exist as my own life. Because I see this, I live through my experience of these things. The reality of all things and the reality of my self are one and the same. When we practice with whatever we encounter as our lives, we finally encounter our true selves.

Further on, Dogen Zenji says:

> However, upon hearing expressions such as *self-verification*, *self-realization*, and so on, stupid people might think that they should study the way by themselves without receiving anything from teachers. This is a great mistake. Those who without transmission from a teacher mistakenly think that their own discriminating thinking is the truth are the same as the non-Buddhists in India who emphasized "naturalness."

Such people live only according to their own limited and immature ideas; they do not study the self in its true meaning.

In my late twenties, when I read Jishozanmai, I decided to leave home and become a monk. I understood that if I lived based only on my thinking, my life would continue to be childish and unenlightened. Since ancient times there have been people who sought the self in its true sense. Unless I wholeheartedly practiced with such a person, one who had truly and completely pursued and clarified the self, I would never be able to understand my true self. When I reached this conclusion, I finally made up my mind to become a monk and practice Zen.

In response to my decision my father said, "You are a critical and argumentative person. It's no good to follow a mediocre teacher," and he tried to find a good master for me. Finally he recommended

Sawaki Roshi, who was then the officer in charge of instructing monks at Sojiji. He told me to go there and, if I thought Sawaki Roshi was a good teacher, to ask about being his disciple.

This was the first time I encountered a person who spoke clearly about the self for which I'd been searching. Although I had listened to many lectures on Buddhism and Christianity, those talks had nothing to do with the self. Sawaki Roshi talked about the self, starting only from the self. I eagerly took notes. When I went home I summarized his teachings according to my notes:

1. The Buddhadharma teaches that this life is our true and final refuge.
2. To practice zazen is to become the transparent self.
3. To practice zazen is the self selfing the self by the self.
4. To practice zazen is to become the self that is connected with the universe.
5. Zazen is good for nothing.

Even though I wrote these before becoming a monk, when I knew nothing about zazen but had only heard Sawaki Roshi's lectures for the first time, I think they're a pretty good summary; I surprised myself. Although I had tentatively made up my mind to become a monk, part of me didn't really want to. I didn't know what kind of physical and mental experiences I would have to go through as a monk, so deep in my mind I wanted to avoid it. Yet after hearing Sawaki Roshi's teaching, I couldn't avoid it anymore. I'd reached the point where I felt that if I wanted to live based on the truth of the self, I couldn't escape. So I was ordained.

1. The Buddhadharma teaches that this life is our true and final refuge.

As I said, my youthful wish was to live the truth. But what is the truth? That was something I couldn't clearly understand. Sawaki Roshi expressed it as "having reached the place we need to reach." After hearing only this single expression, I resolved to become his disciple.

In Sawaki Roshi's phrase, most people live their lives based on "half-baked, bogus, and incomplete views." They never live the ultimate truth of a stable way of life. Since we were born human beings, and this is the only life available, we should live in a true way, constantly refining our lives with this body and mind.

After I became a monk and studied Buddhism, I learned that this expression was not merely Sawaki Roshi's personal opinion; he spoke based on sound authority. In *Shobogenzo Kiesanbo* (or "Taking Refuge in the Three Treasures") we read:

> Question: Why should we take refuge solely in these Three Treasures?

> Reply: Because these three are the ultimate place to return.

The Three Treasures refer to Buddha, Dharma, and Sangha. Why should we take refuge in the Buddha's teaching? Because the Buddha's teaching is where we ultimately return in this human life.

In *Shobogenzo Kesakudoku* (or "Virtue of the Kashaya") we read:

> Their possessions and dwellings are not genuine because they were created by previous karma. Just take refuge in the correctly transmitted Buddhadharma. This is the true place to return for the sake of studying the buddha way.

Our belongings and the world we dwell in are merely the result of our previous karma. We say self-importantly, "From my point of view . . ." but we think as we do only because we're influenced by our conditioning. Thinking based on the past cannot be an ultimate point of view. Dogen Zenji advised us to take refuge in the correctly transmitted Buddhadharma, where the true self returns.

In the constitution established by Prince Shotoku, we read, "We should wholeheartedly respect the Three Treasures. The Three Treasures refer to the Buddha, the Dharma, and the Sangha. These are the final refuge of all four kinds of living beings and the ultimate origin of all countries." The four kinds of living beings include those born of a womb, egg, moisture, and metamorphosis—that is, all living beings. For all living beings, the Three Treasures are the ultimate origin and final refuge.

Sawaki Roshi coined the expression *yukitsukutokoro he yukitsuita jinsei*, or "life in which we have reached the place we need to reach." This phrase summarizes all the expressions used in the excerpts above: the ultimate place to return, the true place to return, the final refuge, and the ultimate origin.

As I said before, people's lives today are based on their random, false, and incomplete views of life. Why do we live this way? Simply by force of habit. This is the stupidity of sleepiness. On the other hand, sometimes we get all caught up in trying to get what we want. That's the stupidity of desire.

Sawaki Roshi often talked about "group stupidity." This refers to the activities of people who pursue something that's important to a group they identify with. There are various forms of group stupidity. There are salaried workers who live only to labor for the benefit of their companies. That's the stupidity of organization. Other people live only for the sake of some "ism" or ideology. That's the stupidity of argument. Many people think they must compete with each other to survive. They force their children to study harder and harder, so they can be "winners" in the struggle. That's the stupidity of competition.

All these people live according to their random, false, and incomplete views of life. The important thing is to start from the self and live a true way of life. This must be the foundation of everything else.

2. To practice zazen is to become the transparent self.

There are various ways to practice zazen. The essence of Dogen Zenji's zazen is being transparent. In one of the new religions in Japan, *Seicho-No-Ie,* people practice a kind of meditation called "contemplation of God." During their meditation, they visualize themselves as children of God and ask Him to cure their illnesses. This kind of practice is colored by a desire for healing. If we practice zazen to gain enlightenment, zazen is colored by that desire. Dogen Zenji's zazen must be colorless and clear.

What is the transparent practice of zazen? In *Fukanzazengi,* Dogen wrote, "Think of not-thinking. How do you think of not-thinking? Beyond thinking."

In our minds, various thoughts are always arising. These are based on discrimination. What we think isn't true because it's a continuation of past karma. Does this mean we should strive to eliminate thoughts? Is the condition of "no thinking" the true reality of our life? It is not! As long as we're alive, thoughts never cease. But if we chase after them, we're merely thinking; we're not practicing zazen.

Needless to say, zazen is not thinking. Neither is it being without thoughts. If I become a vegetable, I might have no thoughts at all, but this cannot be the true reality of human life. The point is to be transparent and allow thoughts to come freely, without trying to eliminate them. When they go, let them go. Don't pursue them. This is the essential point of zazen taught by Dogen Zenji. He said in *Shobogenzo Zuimonki*, "Zazen is nothing but the true form of the Self."

Dogen Zenji expressed the transparency of zazen with the phrase "undefiled practice-verification." To be undefiled is extremely difficult. If I say I'm not defiled, I'm already defiled. If I say I want to become transparent, I'm far from transparency. Colorlessness, transparency, and purity are very difficult to realize.

I'll discuss this again when I take up the fifth statement: "Zazen is good for nothing."

3. To practice zazen is the self selfing the self by the self.

For a long time I wasn't sure I understood this saying. Eventually, it became clear that it means living out the reality of the true self. To live the reality of the self is to see the value of the self within the self.

In 1969 an American visited me. He was the president of a big company. "I have a good family," he said. "I'm wealthy, but I can't help feeling empty and lonely these days. Why is this so?" I replied, "It's because you don't know who you really are. You're not actualizing your true self."

Ordinarily, you see your self as a parent, in relation to your children, or a husband or wife, in relation to your spouse. At work, you define yourself in terms of your position. Within your company, you're a subordinate in relation to your superior, a boss to your subordinates. You're a salesman in relation to your customers. Compared to a highly competent person, you're incapable. You're poor when you compare yourself to a millionaire. You define who you are within relationship or comparison to others. You believe the figure you create this way is your self.

The company president thought of himself as a successful businessman, but that was only an image he created based on his relation to others. When he tried to see himself without comparison to others, he could find nothing definite to refer to as himself, and he suddenly felt empty and lonely. When I told him this, he was impressed and said he would like to practice zazen at Antaiji.

This is an example of someone who discovered the emptiness of his way of life. Most people cling to their image of themselves within relationship to others and never question the true reality of the self. This is how they live without feeling empty.

I heard an interesting story the other day. Someone called a company and asked to speak to Director Tanaka. The person who answered the call said, "Hey, Tanaka, this guy wants to speak with Director Tanaka!" Actually Tanaka wasn't a director, only a section head. However, when he took the call, Tanaka's voice sounded pleased because the caller referred to him as a director. This is an example of someone who mistakes a position for himself. He believes the judgments of others prove his value.

As written in the Sutta Nipata, "One who relies on others is always vacillating." As long as you rely on others, you're conditioned by them. When they change, you have to change.

For example, suppose you have a certain amount of wealth and expect to live comfortably after retirement. However, the value of your money decreases year after year. Now you can't help being upset when you think about the future. You think perhaps your children will take care of you when you're old, but it's not certain they can afford to. You realize you can't rely on your money or your children. There are many such examples in this world.

In contrast, there's a story about Shakyamuni Buddha's final days, when he was very old. On his last journey, attended only by Ananda, he became sick. The Buddha said, "I'm tired. Please prepare a place for me to lie down." Ananda made a bed in the shade of a big tree and the Buddha lay down to rest. After a while, he recovered a little, stood up, and began to walk. After a short distance, he again said, "I'm tired," and lay down. Ananda became worried and wanted to summon the other disciples, but the Buddha didn't allow it. As his last teaching, the Buddha offered the following words: "Take refuge in the self. Take refuge in the Dharma. Do not take refuge in anything else."

In Kaviratna's translation of the Dhammapada we read, "The self is the master of the self. Who else can that master be? With the self fully subdued, one obtains the sublime refuge, which is difficult to achieve."

To be settled in the self is the basis of Buddha's teaching. This is expressed by Sawaki Roshi as "the self selfing the self" and by Dogen Zenji as "the samadhi of the self." This is the foundation of their teachings.

When I began sesshin at Antaiji after Sawaki Roshi passed away, I decided to wholeheartedly carry out his teaching by giving it the fullest possible expression.

While Roshi was alive, we got up in the morning and sat one or two periods and then chanted sutras. After that, we had breakfast, then cleaned and drank tea. After tea we went back to the zendo, and after a while, heard a lecture. We did many things mixed with zazen, which is generally what sesshins are like.

However, I began a kind of sesshin in which we only sit zazen, without doing anything else. We have three meals, and after eating we do *kinhin*, walking meditation. We just repeat zazen and kinhin all day long, from four in the morning until nine in the evening without interruption. No social interaction. No speaking. No relationship to others.

We don't use the *kyosaku*, the hitting stick. If you sit only one or two periods, it's good to hit people with the kyosaku to wake them. But when you sit all day, being the self without relationship to others, it's impossible to sleep from beginning to end for five days. Eventually you wake up. When you wake up, you sit seriously because you practice only for yourself, not for others.

The kyosaku can also become a kind of toy; people start to play with it, thinking, "He hit me. When it's my turn to hold the stick, I'll hit him back." We put such emotions into zazen because we're ordinary sentient beings. So we don't use the kyosaku. We just sit together wholeheartedly as our practice. We sit zazen and do the self by the self with the self.

This practice is not limited to sesshin; throughout our lives we should live as if facing the wall. This has been my practice. I became a disciple of Sawaki Roshi in 1941 and followed him for twenty-five years until his death in 1965. During that time I never received a salary. I wasn't paid even one yen. I never got a bonus, retirement package, or pension. I didn't get a priest's license. I encourage my disciples to practice the same way. No matter how long they stay at Antaiji, they'll never get a license, salary, or pension. Yet I ask them to go on practicing zazen silently for ten years.

In the common style of practice, monks sometimes complain about the hard time they have: sitting diligently for a few years in extreme conditions such as cold, perhaps getting hit often with the kyosaku. However, that way of practice—using hardships as toys and with the reward of a certificate at the end—is very incomplete. Our simple practice for decades with no toys or rewards is the most severe.

I became a monk when I was thirty. By the time I was forty, my friends from elementary school, middle school, and university had high positions in society. I used to beg in Takatsuki, a city halfway between Kyoto and Osaka. A friend from Waseda University was the mayor there. I'll never forget that. I begged and received small coins one by one in the streets of the city where my old friend was the mayor. Now he's a member of the national House of Councilors or something like that.

Another friend from middle school was the factory manager at Mitsubishi in Kyoto; he was in charge of five thousand workers. I practiced as a novice monk until I was fifty-five years old. I had only small jobs, like cooking rice in the temple kitchen. An entire life based on practicing zazen for decades with no bait is facing the wall every moment. From the perspective of human sentiment, this is a severe practice.

Nonetheless, I tell my disciples they should sit silently for ten years. Several have already sat that long. Now I tell them, "Sit silently for ten more years." When they've sat for twenty years, I'll say, "Sit another ten." If I told them at the beginning to sit for thirty years, they would be astonished. So first I tell them to sit for ten years, then ten more. If they sit for twenty years, another ten won't be difficult, because by then they'll have confidence. If they sit for thirty years, people who started in their twenties will be in their fifties. If they sit immovably, without any bait, until they're fifty years old, I'm sure they'll become capable of carrying out great work.

It's wonderful to continue sitting wholeheartedly with no bait. Why? When one just sits facing the wall for twenty or thirty years, one actualizes the self that's only the self without relation to others; one finds the value of the self within the self. If one doesn't find this value, it's impossible to continue sitting.

Ordinarily, people think their value is based on the judgments of others. They find their worth in the size of their salaries. If they become something like a section chief or director at work, they think they're important. If they own a business, they think they become more valuable when sales increase. In actuality, they're merely playing with toys.

Right now, stop playing—sit as the self that is only the self without comparison to others. To practice zazen is the self selfing the self. This means to find one's value as a person within the self and live the reality of life. This is the foundation of the samadhi of the self.

4. To practice zazen is to become the self that is connected with the universe.

Usually, we assume that we know who we are. But the self we think we understand is the self in relation to others. And there are so many different others.

There are billions of human beings on earth at this moment; I'm only one of them. If we calculate the number of human beings in the past and future, I'm one out of innumerable others.

Recently, I read in the newspaper something like the following: You have two parents. Your parents have two parents each. If you count your total ancestors for forty generations, their numbers become over a trillion. If we assume one generation is thirty years, this takes us back around twelve hundred years. It's amazing to realize there are billions and billions of ancestors in such a short period.

And that's only humans. If we include all living beings on earth, "others" are countless. The earth is only one planet in a solar system that's part of a much larger galactic system. There are two hundred billion permanent stars in our galaxy alone, and there are googols of galactic systems in the known universe. In relation to others, I amount to nearly nothing.

Each of us as an individual is only a tiny fraction of the universe: $1/\text{everything}$. We may carelessly kill ants by stepping on them, but we're no larger than an ant, really.

Sometimes politicians say human life is more valuable than anything. They say beautiful things to win our hearts. However, it's a mistake to believe them; they don't actually believe themselves. If a world war breaks out, they could draft you into service simply by sending you a postcard—telling you your life is worth the cost of a postcard stamp. At least this is some value. But in reality, I, out of a googol of beings, have no more value than an E. coli bacterium. "All beings" is truly boundless and infinite.

And yet all beings exist to me because I experience them as my life. The life experience of the self is the basis of the self's conception of everything. In mathematics, $1 = 1/1 = 2/2 = 3/3 = \ldots \; {}^{\text{everything}}/_{\text{everything}}$. The self must be ${}^{\text{everything}}/_{\text{everything}}$.

For you, this world exists only because you're alive. All beings exist because the self exists. Therefore, each of us is living the life that is ${}^{\text{everything}}/_{\text{everything}}$, everything out of everything. At the same time, we live as individuals, as $1/\text{everything}$. The self is a wondrous thing.

To practice zazen is the self that is $1/\text{everything}$ being one with the self that is ${}^{\text{everything}}/_{\text{everything}}$. Just as a compass needle always points north, within myself I always face the self that is connected with all things. This is the meaning of "becoming the self that is connected with the universe." When I speak of the theory, this is it. However, what does this mean as reality? How do we actually feel this?

One year at Antaiji, one of my disciples made a flowerbed and planted a lot of tulips. When spring came the tulips sprouted, grew buds, and bloomed in many colors. There were red, yellow, blue, purple, black, and orange ones. All were very brightly colored, as if painted with enamel. They were beautiful!

One warm and peaceful spring day, I looked at them and thought, "How do all these different colors come out of the same soil?" It was amazing. After a while I had a realization. Those colors didn't come only from the soil. The tulips absorbed carbon dioxide from the air, along with the light and warmth of the sun. Even a tiny tulip blossoms out of the whole heaven and earth. I felt this deeply.

Another day that spring, I watched clouds drifting peacefully across the sky. I was moved and composed a poem:

CLOUDS—A POEM OF LIFE

Clouds
suddenly appear out of the whole heaven and earth
and disappear into the whole heaven and earth.

Floating aimlessly with a smile,
some flow peacefully and quietly.
Others evolve mountainously and laugh loudly,
still others invite thunder and roar.
Spring clouds rain and quietly moisten the earth.
Monsoon clouds sweep over with a long spell of rain.
Snow clouds feel remorse in winter's deep silence.
Typhoons filled with hatred run wild.
Blizzard clouds swirl and storms blow
as if trying to kill all beings.
And sometimes,
the clouds all disappear,
leaving only the deep blue sky
that presents no obstacles.

Clouds
suddenly appear out of the whole heaven and earth
and disappear into the whole heaven and earth.
These clouds are
the prototype of all living beings and all existences.
The whole heaven and earth is nothing
but life.

It's very interesting to watch clouds. Each has its unique form of expression. Each takes different shapes. We humans are the same. We are completely like clouds.

Sawaki Roshi once said, "Everyone in this world is just scrambling for clouds." This is true. Money is like clouds. People compete with each other for money and status, but sooner or later it all disappears. People will find they've only been scrambling for clouds.

However, we should understand that the foundation from which all cloud-like things appear is the life of the whole heaven and earth. A little later I wrote this poem on the *nembutsu*, the primary mantra of Shin Buddhists:

THE HEART OF NEMBUTSU

I eat food from the whole heaven and earth.
I drink water from the whole heaven and earth.
I breathe air from the whole heaven and earth.
I live the life of the whole heaven and earth.
Pulled by the gravity
of the whole heaven and earth,
I become pure and clear, one with the whole heaven and
    earth.
The whole heaven and earth is where I return.

The food we eat—radishes, carrots, greens, rice, meat—all appears out of the whole heaven and earth. We drink water from the whole heaven and earth. We breathe air from the whole heaven and earth. We live the life that permeates the whole heaven and earth. Everything without exception arises from the whole heaven and earth. We are pulled by the gravity of the whole heaven and earth. We become free of clinging to our selves and become one with the whole heaven and earth. The whole heaven and earth is where we return.

This whole heaven and earth is called Amitabha, meaning "infinite life" or "light." Food, air, water—anything and everything is a gift from Amitabha. This is Amitabha's original vow. We are living the life of Amitabha as a function of the gravitational force of this vow. Drawn by this vow, I become pure and clear, one with Amitabha. In

Buddhism, faith, or *shin*, means being pure and clear. Pulled by the magnetic force of the whole heaven and earth, we become pure and clear together with the whole heaven and earth. This is Buddhist faith.

The nembutsu begins with *namu*, which means "returning to life." That is, we return to our true life, to the self that is connected with the universe. The foundation of practice taught by Dogen Zenji is the same. We are constantly functioning as the life of the whole heaven and earth.

The whole mantra is *Namu Amida Butsu*, which means "taking refuge in Amitabha Buddha"—Amida is the Japanese name of Amitabha.

NAMU AMIDA BUTSU

Amida is "infinite."
Wherever, whatever happens,
it takes place within my life.
Namu is "to return to life,"
paying no attention
to what I might think
or what I might believe,
being pulled
by the gravitational force
of the absolute reality
that is my life.
Through body, speech, and mind
always here and now
functioning with
Namu-amida.
This is called *Butsu*.
Butsu is a mature human being.

Amitabha doesn't exist because I believe he exists. Amitabha Buddha exists without being concerned whether I believe in him or not. Regardless what I think or believe, Amitabha is the whole heaven and earth. Being pulled by Amitabha's original vow that is the absolute reality, I function through my own body, speech, and mind as all-pervading self. This is being a buddha—a great being, a truly mature person.

Everyone smiles when their desires are fulfilled and complains when things go against their wishes. Even when we're physically mature, humans tend to be childish, always hungry and wanting more. Spiritually we never evolve beyond this condition. A person who's only physically mature is a fake adult.

To be a buddha is to be a mature human instead of a phony adult like a hungry ghost. Being a buddha is not something special. Dogen Zenji made this clear in *Shobogenzo Hachidainingaku*, or "Eight Aspects of Great Beings' Awakening." Sawaki Roshi's saying that zazen is the posture of being connected with the universe is the same. Practice as taught by Dogen Zenji is simply becoming an adult in the true meaning of the word.

In short, zazen is to stop doing—to face the wall and sit, just being the self that is only the self. In zazen, we should refrain from doing anything else. Yet being human we begin to think things. Then we begin to converse and interact with our thoughts.

If you're a stockbroker you might think, "I should have sold the shares then. No, I should've bought," or "I should have waited." If you're a young lover, you might find your girlfriend appears in your mind all the time. If you're a mother who doesn't get along with her daughter-in-law, you might think only of your son's wife. In zazen, while you're supposed to be doing nothing, thoughts will arise of their own accord in relation to whatever life situation you're in.

And yet, when you realize you're thinking and return to just sitting, the thoughts that appeared before you like images on TV suddenly disappear, as if you had switched the television off. Only the wall is left in front of you—for an instant, that's it. Then thoughts arise. You return to zazen, and they vanish. We simply repeat this. Awareness of reality is called *kakusoku*. This is zazen. The most important point is to keep repeating this kakusoku billions of times. This is how we should practice.

If we practice like this we can't help but realize our thoughts are nothing but secretions of the brain. Just as our salivary glands secrete saliva and our stomachs secrete gastric juices, our brains secrete thoughts. However, usually we don't understand this. When we think, "I hate him!" we despise the person, forgetting that this thought is merely a secretion. Hatred occupies our mind, tyrannizing it. By hating, we subordinate ourselves to this tyrant. When we love someone, we're swept away by our attachment; we become enslaved by love. In the end, all of us live as serfs to this lord: thought. This is the source of our problems.

Our stomachs secrete gastric juices to digest food. More isn't better; if too much is secreted, the acid damages the stomach wall, and we develop ulcers. While our stomachs secrete enzymes to keep us alive, excess can be dangerous. Nowadays, we suffer from an excess of brain secretions and allow ourselves to be tyrannized by them. This is the cause of our mistakes.

In reality, the thoughts arising in our minds are nothing but the scenery of the life of the self. We shouldn't be blind to or unconscious of this scenery. We need to see it clearly; zazen commands a view of everything. In ancient Zen texts, this is called "the scenery of the original ground."

Our practice isn't how we become the interpenetrating life of the whole heaven and earth; now and always, that is how we are. Yet even though we're connected with the whole universe, we don't manifest this in our lives. Because our minds constantly discriminate, we chase the tails of our brains' secretions. When we do zazen, we let go of thoughts and they fall away. What arises in our minds disappears. Then interpenetrating life manifests itself as the whole heaven and earth.

Dogen Zenji called this "practice based on verification." Universe-full life is itself verification. We practice the whole universe. Practice and verification are one.

We all prefer happiness to misery, heaven to hell, survival to death. We're thus forever bifurcating reality, dividing it into good and bad, like and dislike. We discriminate between realization and delusion and strive to attain realization. In attempting to gain something desirable, we're already unstable. When we strive for enlightenment, we're deluded because of our desire to escape our present condition. But the reality of the universe lies far beyond attraction and aversion. When our attitude is "whichever, whatever, wherever," we manifest the whole heaven and earth.

Dogen Zenji taught that our attitude should be diligent practice in every situation we encounter. If we fall into hell, we just practice there and go through hell; this is the most important attitude to have. When we encounter an unfortunate situation, we work through it with sincerity. Just sit in the reality of life, seeing heaven and hell, misery and joy, life and death, with the same eye. No matter what the situation, we live the life of the self there. We sit immovably on that foundation. This is being connected with the universe. This is how we practice the self selfing the self. The life that permeates the entire universe, the whole heaven and earth, is where we finally return.

5. Zazen is good for nothing.

Sawaki Roshi once ended a long talk on zazen by saying it was good for nothing. People might have thought he was joking, but he wasn't.

As I've said, whatever happens, I live out my life. As long as I maintain this attitude, I can't go anywhere else; there's nowhere to go. Since I'm already where I should be, it's natural to say zazen is good for nothing. There's nothing to gain from zazen because we're already filled with the universe.

Shortly after I began to practice with Sawaki Roshi, we were walking in Utsunomiya and I said, "As you know, I'm a rather weak-minded person, but I want to continue to practice zazen with you for twenty or even thirty years, or until you die. If I do that, will it be possible for a weak person like me to become a little stronger?"

Sawaki Roshi replied, "No! Zazen is good for nothing." He had a loud, deep voice and was powerful and resolute. He wasn't a weak yet handsome person like me! He was the traditional image of a Zen monk. "I'm not like this because of my practice," he continued. "I was like this before I began to practice. Zazen doesn't change a person. Zazen is good for nothing."

When I heard those words I thought, "Although he says it isn't possible, still, I'll be able to improve myself." I followed him and practiced zazen for twenty-five years, until his death in December 1965. While he was alive, I relied on him. After he died, I couldn't do that anymore. Just after his death, I recalled my question during our walk and asked myself, "Have I changed after practicing zazen with the roshi for twenty-five years?" I realized I hadn't really changed at all.

In that moment it was natural for me to say to myself, "A violet blooms as a violet, a rose blooms as a rose." There are people like Sawaki Roshi who resemble luxurious roses. There are people like me who resemble tiny, pretty violets. Which is better? It's not a relevant question. We shouldn't compare with others. It's enough to blossom wholeheartedly, just as we are. That's what I felt after Sawaki Roshi died.

In conclusion, I'm living out the life of the whole heaven and earth, the absolute reality, regardless of whether I accept or reject it. The point of our practice is to manifest this life suffusing the whole heaven and earth, here and now. In this practice, there's no judgment of success or failure. If there's success and failure, I'm comparing myself. Since everything I encounter is part of my life, I shouldn't treat anything without respect. I should take care of everything wholeheartedly. I practice this way. Everything I encounter is my life.

"As the person realizes one dharma, the person penetrates one dharma; as the person encounters one practice, the person fully practices one practice," Dogen Zenji wrote in *Shobogenzo Genjokoan*. When I encounter one thing, I practice one thing.

For example, when we climb a mountain, we climb moment by moment, one step at a time. It's not that we climb a mountain only when we reach the summit. To advance one step at a time is what's important. We live moment by moment, step by step. This is the activity of the whole heaven and earth. It's an activity that's good for nothing. It's practice-enlightenment without defilement.

According to *Shobogenzo Yuibutsuyobutsu*, or "Only a Buddha Together with a Buddha," being *undefiled* means neither accepting nor rejecting. There's nothing to pick up or throw away. There's nowhere to go. Since everything is the whole heaven and earth, it cannot be defiled. With this pure life force, continue to live here and now, manifesting the whole heaven and earth.

Simply doing this practice that's good for nothing is the meaning of *shikan*, or "just." Dogen Zenji often used this word as "just doing" or "doing single-mindedly." This doesn't mean experiencing ecstasy or becoming absorbed in some activity. To experience ecstasy or absorption, an object is needed. Shikan has no object. It's *just doing* as the pure life force of the self.

In our modern world, most people think of their lives in terms of competition with others in a struggle for existence, money, status, or power. But a true way of life has nothing to do with competition. We are the self that is only the self. We do the self that is connected with the whole universe. Whoever and whatever I encounter is my life. We just do things with the pure life force of the self and without expectation. We actually want to live out such a self. We don't have to weep when we fail or fall behind in some kind of competition. There's no need to pursue or escape because of a desire to gain happiness or reject sadness. If we restlessly run after or away from things, this way and that, our lives are always unstable.

Living straightforwardly with a dignified attitude, moved by the life force of the self that is connected with the whole universe—this is life based on the zazen that Dogen Zenji and Sawaki Roshi taught.

Recollections of My Teacher, Kodo Sawaki Roshi
by Kosho Uchiyama

Kodo Sawaki Roshi is commonly acknowledged as the driving force behind restoring the practice of shikantaza, or just sitting, within Soto Zen, the tradition founded by Dogen Zenji. The goal of this practice is not some special enlightenment separate from sitting. Because of this "nothing special" attitude, even people in the Soto school didn't take zazen seriously for a long time before Sawaki Roshi appeared.

These days, many scholars outside Soto study Dogen Zenji's *Shobogenzo*. As a result, people have begun to recognize the profundity of shikantaza. Also, young Soto priests have begun holding summer zazen gatherings all over Japan. Many temples now have regular sitting groups and are qualified as practice centers by Soto headquarters. However, before people became interested in Dogen's Zen, from the beginning of the Showa era, Sawaki Roshi practiced zazen without satori and widely encouraged others to practice. Because of Sawaki Roshi's lifelong work, many people practice zazen today.

Sawaki Roshi often said, "Dogen Zenji's zazen is very profound. Childish people can't aspire to practice it." Indeed, Dogen Zenji's zazen can be practiced only by those who tackle questions about their own lives.

In the future, Japanese society may become materially rich. Feelings of emptiness caused by this materialistic existence will arise in many people's hearts, and they'll begin to practice zazen.

In the past, Japanese people had to think first of their livelihood, so few could consider the meaning of their lives. Koans were therefore given to people inspired to practice Zen. They practiced zazen only as a method of breaking through these koans. So zazen was carried out more by koan practitioners than those in the Soto Zen tradition.

Because people who wanted to practice usually went to Rinzai temples and studied koans, it must have been difficult initially to encourage people to just sit. However, because of his charisma, unique karmic attributes, and the power of his own diligent practice, Sawaki Roshi successfully achieved this mission.

Wherever he went, people were attracted to him like iron to a magnet. Sometimes the force of his personality could be overpowering. For instance, when he said, "Zazen is good for nothing," people were caught by his personality and thought, "Even though Roshi says this in words, zazen must bring us some benefit." Although he convinced people to sit, they didn't always understand why.

Sawaki Roshi practiced more conscientiously than anyone. I became his disciple at Daichuji temple in Tochigi Prefecture on December 8, 1941. At the time, he was in his sixties, and during sesshin at Daichuji the wake-up bell rang at 2:50 a.m. But Roshi started to sit at 1:30. We sat until 10 p.m. He slept only a few hours a night. He practiced this way for five days each month, as well as one week during Rohatsu, the celebration of Buddha's enlightenment.

When he saw practitioners slack off even a little, he scolded and goaded us with his thunderous voice, as if the huge temple building were shaking. Drawn by his power, practitioners were able to just sit the zazen that has nothing to do with satori, that is in fact very dissatisfactory.

Practice at Daichuji ended in the fall of 1944, and Sawaki Roshi's disciples had no place to stay. Until 1949, when we settled at Antaiji in Kyoto, we had to move around. I remember Sawaki Roshi walking alongside his disciples and saying, "This is a Dharma challenge."

Finally we settled at Antaiji. At the beginning of our time there, he still sometimes thundered at us. However, around 1952 or 1953, I said to him, "We left home and became monks after arousing bodhi mind. We're practicing zazen seriously. Please don't worry. We'll practice even if you don't scold us." After that, he never shouted at Antaiji. He changed his attitude very quickly. That was typical of him.

And yet, at Komazawa University and other places, it seemed he continued shouting until he stopped teaching. Once, a student who visited Antaiji said with wonder, "I can't believe the Sawaki Roshi I meet at Komazawa and at Antaiji are the same person." Practitioners at Antaiji had a very different view of Roshi than his other students. This multifaceted personality is who Sawaki Roshi was.

Relatively speaking, Sawaki Roshi was a good-natured old man at Antaiji. By relaxing his authority, he taught us that zazen is the "most honored one" and we could practice more spontaneously, from our own motivation rather than external pressure.

I've stayed at Antaiji since his death and maintained the zazen practice here. During this period, a weak-minded person like me has been able to serve as abbot without letting Antaiji decline. This is completely due to the support of many people. I deeply appreciate it. At the same time, it's also because Sawaki Roshi left me the advice, "Zazen is the most honored one." I'd like to express my infinite gratitude to Sawaki Roshi's teachings. I'm determined to cherish his counsel always. I also hope later generations continue his teaching.

Viewing zazen as the most honored one determines our attitude toward our whole lives. What should our outlook be? Here is my best attempt to express what my teacher inscribed in my mind.

- Gaining is delusion and losing is realization.
- Don't try to get any benefit. Don't be greedy; don't regret losing.
- Never establish an organization. Things achieved by an institution will collapse because of that institution. This rise and fall of accomplishments is nothing other than transmigration within samsara. This was Sawaki Roshi's fundamental attitude.
- Teach individuals one by one. Rather than educating people generally within a system, we need to address each individually, since each is unique.
- Don't ask for donations. People have the idea that if they're involved in a temple, they'll be asked to donate. This has seriously injured Buddhadharma. We never ask for donations. That way people can come without worrying about money.
- Don't be fickle. Don't act pulled by your self-centered thoughts.
- If you're careless, you'll become famous and achieve a high position. Make every effort not to rise in the world. Particularly after age forty, fame and profit will be tempting.

Each of these sayings, at first glance, sounds straightforward. Yet when you look closely, you'll find they're not the mainstream teachings of this world. Sawaki Roshi not only taught these sayings, he manifested them as an example.

Because I practiced with him intimately for twenty-five years, until his final days, these teachings have been engraved within me. Whenever I encounter trouble, they come to mind, and I feel my teacher is still instructing me. I'm deeply grateful for this.

> Only this ground of three feet square.
> No matter how much I use, this ground is inexhaustible over my entire life.
> My teacher transmitted only this ground of zazen that is three feet square.
> I take refuge in my original teacher, Somon Kodo Daiosho.

The Life of Homeless Kodo
by Shohaku Okumura

Childhood: Experiencing Impermanence and Getting Tougher

Kodo Sawaki Roshi was born June 16, 1880, in Tsu, Mie Prefecture; his given name was Saikichi. He was the sixth child of Sotaro and Shige Tada. His father made rickshaw parts. His mother died when he was four, and his father died three years later.

By the time his father passed away, three of Saikichi's siblings had already died; the four remaining children were adopted separately. Saikichi was adopted by his aunt Hiino, though her husband wasn't happy about this. He once served Saikichi rice and eggplant so old it was almost black. Saikichi said, "I don't like such old eggplant." His uncle answered, "Then don't eat," and took Saikichi's food away. For the rest of his life, Saikichi never expressed preferences about food.

In August, Hiino's husband died suddenly of a stroke in front of Saikichi, who was then adopted by Bunkichi Sawaki, a lantern maker living in Isshinden, Tsu. The boy's name became Saikichi Sawaki.

Bunkichi was a gambler, and his wife was a former prostitute. The couple lived in a red-light district. One day a middle-aged man died of a stroke in a prostitute's room nearby. Eight-year-old Saikichi saw the dead man in bed with his wife beside him, crying, "Why did you die in a place like this, of all places?" This scene stunned Saikichi into a deep appreciation of transience and the impossibility of keeping secrets—even when his parents and uncle had died, Saikichi hadn't felt impermanence so intensely.

Walking home from elementary school once after a heavy rain,

Saikichi fell in a puddle and started to cry, expecting someone to help him. Bunkichi found him but instead of helping slapped his face and said, "What a weakling!" Saikichi realized crying wouldn't help and gradually began becoming tougher.

Saikichi befriended Iwakichi Morita, the son of a paper craftsman in the neighborhood. He found this family very different from his. Iwakichi's father taught his son and Saikichi classic Chinese texts. Iwakichi also studied Japanese painting, later becoming a painter. He told Saikichi many stories about artists with no desire for wealth or fame. Under the influence of this family, Saikichi began to understand there were more important things in the world than fame and money, and he aspired to find such a way of life. This idea caused conflict with his adoptive parents; his life with them was very different. They forced him to sell snacks in their gambling den and keep a lookout for the police.

Early Teens: Anguish

At twelve Saikichi graduated from elementary school and began to work as a lantern maker. His parents relied on his earnings, but Saikichi's angst deepened because of the contradiction between his circumstances and his aspiration to focus on things other than money.

He often visited a Pure Land Buddhist temple to listen to the priest's sermons. He was struck by the story of the boy named Snow Mountain, who offered his life to a monster when he heard the verse of truth.

One day when Saikichi was walking with his adoptive father, they came across a fight. About seventy gangsters were fighting with swords. The leader of one side was Bunkichi's relative. Although Bunkichi usually looked tough, this time he was paralyzed with fear. That night, Bunkichi was ordered to take a message to one of the gangsters who escaped into the mountains, but he was too afraid. Saikichi volunteered for the job, walking about fifteen miles alone in the dark. After that, Bunkichi never hit him.

Leaving Home: Searching for a Teacher

Saikichi started to think of becoming a Buddhist monk, but he questioned whether he should give up his responsibility to support his adoptive parents. At fifteen, he ran away to Osaka. He wanted to earn some money for his parents and then become a monk. His parents found him and took him back.

However, his desire to be a monk grew stronger. When he confided this wish, the local Pure Land priest suggested he become a Zen monk. Saikichi left home and walked for four days to Eiheiji, one of the two head monasteries of Sotoshu. He asked the temple to ordain him, but he was refused; to practice at Eiheiji, people first needed to find a master and ordain as a monk.

Saikichi said, "I can't go back. I'm too hungry to walk. Let me die here." The monk said, "I'll give you some rice porridge. Eat it and go." Saikichi answered, "Then I don't need food."

He stayed at the gate for two days without eating. The work leader finally allowed him in and arranged for him to stay as a lay worker. Someone made a robe for him out of abandoned robes. He was very happy. The monks seemed like bodhisattvas to him.

He was taught how to sit zazen. One day when he went to storage for some sugar, he saw the shadows of several monks in zazen. He was struck by something like an electric shock and started to walk carefully, without making noise. This was his first experience of feeling zazen was sacred.

Another time, he was sent with several training monks to assist at a big ceremony at Ryuunji temple. After the ceremony, the priests went out to have fun, while Saikichi stayed at the temple and sat zazen. While he was sitting, an old woman accidentally came into the room. When she saw the sixteen-year-old lay worker sitting, she bowed reverently, as if he were a buddha. She was a bossy woman who usually treated Saikichi like a servant. Although he knew nothing about the meaning of zazen, these experiences convinced him it was worth practicing.

Although he tried to find a priest near Eiheiji who would ordain him, he was not successful. In January he left Eiheiji and walked to Soshinji in Kumamoto Prefecture, Kyushu, to visit Rev. Koho Sawada. He had no money, and he encountered many obstacles on this expedition, including being suspected as a pickpocket and jailed for a month. He finally arrived at Soshinji in March.

On December 8, 1897, he was ordained by Rev. Sawada. His Dharma name was Kodo, or Cultivating the Way. He practiced at Soshinji as a novice monk for two years. Rev. Sawada taught him the basic conduct of a Soto Zen monk, such as how to chant and do ceremonies.

During this period, Kodo heard of a lawsuit caused by a conflict between Dharma brothers over the abbacy of a nearby temple, and he realized that a temple could be an object of greed. Over time he saw many similar problems and finally experienced them himself with the elder Dharma brother from whom he received transmission. These experiences made him resolve never to have a temple.

Practice with Ryoun Fueoka: Entering the World of Dogen

At nineteen Kodo left Soshinji to practice at Entsuji in Hyogo Prefecture. Shortly thereafter he met Rev. Ryoun Fueoka and moved to his temple, Hosenji, in Kyoto Prefecture. Rev. Fueoka had practiced with the great Zen master Bokusan Nishiari for about twenty years.

Rev. Fueoka taught Kodo zazen practice as shikantaza in the tradition of Dogen Zenji. He also gave him private lectures on Dogen Zenji's writings. He advised Kodo that to truly understand shikantaza and the other teachings in *Shobogenzo*, he first needed to study Buddhism in general. Kodo found that zazen as taught by Dogen Zenji was what he had been looking for—a positive and authentic way of life.

Military Service: Experiencing Life and Death

A year later Kodo was drafted and served as a soldier for six years. He was almost killed during the Russo-Japanese War. Afterward, he went back to his hometown to recuperate for about three months. He found his adoptive mother mentally ill. He also discovered that his adoptive father had borrowed and gambled away a large sum on the security of the payment he would receive from the government if his son died in battle. Bunkichi blamed him for returning alive, and Kodo had to repay this debt.

During this period, he studied Yogacara with Rev. Joshin Murase, a Pure Land priest who had studied at Horyuji monastery in Nara.

Studying Buddhism in Poverty

Kodo was discharged from military service in January 1906. That summer, he became head student at Soshinji. On August 30, he received Dharma transmission from Rev. Zenko Sawada, a Dharma heir of Koho Sawada.

After transmission, he returned to his hometown and started to study Buddhism as an auditing student at a Shin Buddhist school in Takada. Since he had to repay his adoptive father's debt, he was exempt from school fees, and he was offered a free room at the school. He studied there for two years.

On the recommendation of Rev. Murase, Kodo started to study Yogacara at Horyuji with the abbot, Rev. Join Saeki. After four years he attained the rank of *Iko*, which is the second-highest position in the Yogacara school and the highest status that priests from other Buddhist schools could reach. Some people encouraged him to become a Yogacara monk, but Kodo wasn't interested. For him studying Yogacara was simply preparation for studying Dogen Zenji's teachings.

Besides studying Yogacara, he read Dogen's writings and practiced zazen. He also taught Dogen's texts to a group of Shingon nuns. From them, he discovered the traditionally sewn *nyohoe* robe taught by Jiun Onko, the eighteenth-century scholar monk of the Shingon Ritsu school. This robe was very similar to the one worn by Ryoun Fueoka. Kodo began to study the nyohoe okesa. He often visited Kokiji, where Jiun lived, to see the thousands of okesa stored there. Later Kodo advocated the importance of nyohoe in Soto.

He was still very poor. He only ate rice, soybeans, and pickles. He studied hard to compete with the students from other Buddhist schools. He often debated and supposedly never lost.

Returning to Dogen's Zen: Quiet Practice without Competition

Kodo considered a few points within Dogen's teachings essential. One was shikantaza, just sitting without any expectation of gaining mind, even for enlightenment.

The second was practicing in harmony without competing with

others. In "Bendoho" (or "The Model for Engaging the Way") in *Dogen's Pure Standards*, Dogen wrote:

> In activity and stillness at one with the community, throughout deaths and rebirths do not separate from the monastery. Standing out has no benefit; being different from others is not our conduct. This is the buddhas' and ancestors' skin, flesh, bones, and marrow, and also one's body and mind dropped off.

The third essential point was Dogen's comment in Gakudoyojin-shu (or "Points to Watch in Studying the Way") in *Heart of Zen*:

> It is certainly difficult to mount an effort in one's practice strong enough to break bones and crush marrow. But harmonizing your mind is even more difficult. It is also difficult to observe such precepts as taking only one meal a day, but regulating your actions is the most difficult. Shall we place importance on bone-breaking practice? Though there have been many who have persevered through hardships, few of them have attained the Dharma. Shall we put value on observing the precepts? Though there have been many who did so in the past, few of them realized the Way. This is because harmonizing the mind is extremely difficult. Neither intelligence nor broad knowledge is of primary importance. Intellect, volition, consciousness, memory, imagination, and contemplation are of no value. Without resorting to these methods, enter the buddha-way by harmonizing body and mind.

Kodo was good at winning, and he always worked hard. When young, he was proud of these qualities, but later when he came to deeply appreciate Dogen's teaching, he felt small. At seventy-three, he said he practiced as though scolded by Dogen Zenji. Understanding Dogen's teaching was different from studying Yogacara, in which he accumulated bricks of knowledge. Dogen directly addressed Kodo's attitude toward his life and the Dharma.

In the spring, Kodo visited Eiheiji to attend a one-month *genzoe*, a retreat dedicated to studying Dogen Zenji's teachings. After six years of studying Buddhism, he thought he was ready to explore *Shobogenzo*. As preparation, he studied as many commentaries as possible, especially *Shobogenzo Monge*—a commentary traditionally attributed to Menzan Zuiho but more recently believed to be by Menzan's Dharma grandson, Fusan Gentotsu.

Kodo was very happy to enter the world of Dogen Zenji. In December, he left Horyuji. He was invited to serve as the instructor for apprentice monks at Yosenji monastery in Matsusaka, Mie Prefecture. There he met Rev. Kozan Kato, who was chief cook and later became an eminent Rinzai master. They met again in Kyushu and continued to be friends until the end of their lives. Both Kodo and Kozan were disappointed by Yosenji because the monks there weren't inspired to practice and study Dharma; they only wanted to learn to do ceremonies.

In May 1913, Kodo visited Shoboji in Nara, which had a three-month summer practice period with Sotan Oka Roshi as visiting teacher. With Oka Roshi, Kodo studied *Shobogenzo* and walking meditation. He met many of Oka Roshi's students, including Kyugaku Oka, Eko Hashimoto (Dainin Katagiri Roshi's teacher), Hozen Hosotani, and Ian Kishizawa (who taught Shunryu Suzuki Roshi). While teaching at Yosenji, Kodo often traveled to practice events led by Oka Roshi.

Around this time, Kodo's adoptive father Bunkichi died at the age of sixty-eight. Kodo had been financially supporting him. Kodo once said to him, "Please take this money. When I see your face, I cannot help but become honest and steady. Because of your example, I could not go bad. Please live long." Later Kodo said that his adoptive father had offered preventive medicine against turning bad.

That summer, Kodo and Kozan resolved to leave Yosenji. The day after they made their decision, Kozan was gone. Kodo took longer to depart because he had a huge number of books. Later he said, "That was the only time I was behind others."

Sitting Alone: The House without Anyone in the Empty Eon

Kodo visited Rev. Saeki and asked to live in Jofukuji, a dilapidated branch temple of Horyuji. Rev. Saeki made the arrangements. Kodo sat by himself every day from 2 a.m. to 10 p.m. He ate only rice and pickles. After his experiences at Yosenji, he thought it was impossible to find a sangha that wholeheartedly practiced Dogen Zenji's shikan-taza as the priority of their lives. But this was the way he wanted to practice, even if he did it alone. He found a frame from which the calligraphy had been removed and made his own: "The house without anyone in the empty eon." He hung this where he sat. He practiced like this for more than a year, except when he visited Eiheiji to attend Oka Roshi's Genzoe and other events in Kyoto and Osaka.

Practice at Daijiji: With Friends

In 1916, Oka Roshi was appointed abbot of Daijiji, but he couldn't live there. He asked Kodo to lead the monastery as lecturer, so Kodo went to Daijiji in May. Rev. Hosotani and twenty other training monks were also sent. Kodo had a vigorous practice with them. He was happy to have a community willing to wholeheartedly practice Dogen's shikantaza and other monastic conduct.

Usually they woke at 2 a.m. and sat until 6 a.m. After service, they had breakfast and temple cleaning. In the mornings Kodo lectured on Dogen's writings and Buddhism in general. After noon service and lunch, he taught various aspects of ceremonies, chanting, and other forms. Then they worked until dark. They didn't have time for evening zazen.

During their monthly five-day sesshins, they sat starting at 2 a.m., and they only did zazen, except for three meals followed by thirty minutes of walking meditation. From 4 to 5 p.m. and from midnight to 2 a.m. no one carried the hitting stick. They sat even while sleeping. Kodo would later model the structure of other sesshins on this schedule.

Kodo was invited to the local Fifth High School to give a Dharma talk. After this he visited regularly, and many students were influenced by him. Some came to Daijiji to practice zazen.

Moving to Daitetsudo

On August 11, 1921, Sotan Oka Roshi passed away, and Kodo left Daijiji. Many laypeople, including the governor, donated funds to help him stay in Kumamoto. Kodo was able to rent a house and found a practice center named Daitetsudo, or Great Thoroughness Hall. Many came to sit and listen to his talks. Sometimes people had to sit on the ground in the garden because the zendo was full.

Soshinji temple, where Kodo had been ordained by Rev. Koho Sawada, burned down that year. The temple parishioners wanted Rev. Zenko Sawada to retire and Kodo to become abbot. Rev. Sawada accepted this request. Kodo went to Soshinji and worked to rebuild the temple with the parishioners. But when the reconstruction was complete, the abbot changed his mind and asked Kodo not to take over. Since he didn't want to fight over the temple, Kodo stopped going to Soshinji. This incident solidified his determination not to have a temple.

Mannichi Zan: Beginning the "Moving Monastery"

Because Kodo didn't charge fees, even for meals or overnights, he spent all the donations to Daitetsudo in less than a year and had to leave in 1923. At the end of March, he moved to a second house on Mannichi Zan, a small mountain near Kumamoto station. This house was owned by a Mr. Shibata, a member of the prefectural assembly. He didn't practice, but he respected Kodo very much and offered the house and food free for twelve years. Some people came to sit in the mornings.

Kodo often traveled to lead sesshins or give Dharma talks. He regularly visited places in Saga Prefecture and throughout Kyushu. The circle of his activities was widening. Later he was invited to cities such as Tokyo, Osaka, Nagoya, and Sendai. This was the beginning of his "moving monastery." He continued to live this way for twelve years, until 1935 when he moved to Tokyo to become a professor at Komazawa University.

Nyohoe Movement: Wearing Okesa and Sitting Zazen

In 1931, Kodo was invited to Hoanden Gokokuji in Nagoya for the hundredth anniversary of Zen Master Mokushitsu Ryoyo's death. A former abbot of the temple, Mokushitsu had studied authentic okesa and written the classic *Hobuku Kakusho* (or *Making Correct Dharma Robes*). He was also well known for his study of *Shobogenzo*.

Kodo lectured on *Hobuku Kakusho* and gave a week-long workshop for several hundred people on sewing nyohoe. All the training nuns at the Aichi women's monastery participated in this assembly and sewed nyohoe.

Shortly after, he was invited to the women's monastery to give another nyohoe workshop. Kodo taught Dogen's principle that the okesa and Buddhadharma are not separate. Rev. Genpo Sekido, Dharma descendant of Mokushitsu, participated in this workshop and was impressed by Kodo's teachings. Rev. Sekido and Rev. Eko Hashimoto supported Kodo's nyohoe movement. Because of Kodo's influence, many nuns began to sew nyohoe as their practice; at the women's monastery, all nuns sewed nyohoe as part of their training. This custom continued until 1945.

The nyohoe revival waned because the Soto school headquarters maintained that nyohoe contradicted their regulations regarding vestments. However, in Kodo's and Hashimoto Roshi's lineages, practitioners continued to sew and wear nyohoe.

Today, in the American lineages of Suzuki Roshi, Katagiri Roshi, and Uchiyama Roshi, as well as the European lineage of Deshimaru Roshi, people sew their own nyohoe okesa and rakusu when they ordain as priests. Laypeople similarly sew nyohoe rakusu when they receive the precepts. Kodo was the first to emphasize wearing an authentic okesa.

Moving to Tokyo as a Professor

In April 1935, the president of Komazawa University, Rev. Zenkai Omori, invited Kodo to be a professor there. Although he declined at first, the president persisted. Finally Kodo accepted and moved to Tokyo.

In December he was appointed instructor of apprentice monks at Sojiji, the other main Soto monastery besides Eiheiji. He practiced at Sojiji in the mornings, taught at Komazawa in the afternoons, and led sitting groups at various temples in the evenings.

Kodo became a well-known Zen teacher and his activities grew more extensive. A collection of his Dharma talks, *Zendan* (or *Zen Talks*), was very popular. Although he was busy teaching at Komazawa and

Sojiji, he continued the moving monastery. Whenever he had time, he traveled.

In 1940, Kodo started Tengyo Zenen, or Heavenly Dawn Zen Garden, at Daichuji in Tochigi Prefecture. A few monks lived there. Many priests and laypeople attended Kodo's five-day sesshins. During these he gave lectures, and the schedule included services and work periods.

In other sesshins, the resident monks practiced by themselves. They followed the schedule Kodo had set for sesshins at Daijiji, alternating fifty minutes of zazen with ten minutes of walking meditation from 2 a.m. until midnight. They took turns carrying the stick, except from midnight to two, when they slept sitting on their cushions. This sesshin was called *sannai,* which means "for temple residents."

In the autumn of 1944, Tengyo Zenen closed when elementary school children were evacuated there from Tokyo. Kodo's disciples lost their temple and had to move from place to place for five years.

Antaiji: Final Temple for Homeless Kodo

Kyoto's Antaiji had been founded in 1921 on a layperson's vow to help cultivate eminent scholars and masters who could expound Soto Zen teachings in modern society. Sotan Oka Roshi was invited as the founding abbot. Unfortunately, after the opening ceremony, Oka Roshi became sick, passing away several months later. Rev. Zuirin Odagaki, brother of the founding patron, served as the second abbot.

Antaiji was a study monastery. A few select graduates from Komazawa were allowed to stay there to study Dogen Zenji's teachings. Many students who later became well-known Soto scholars and masters studied at Antaiji before the war, including Kodo Krebayashi (the president of Komazawa University) and Renpo Niwa (the abbot of Eiheiji).

After World War II, Antaiji lost its financial backing, and no priests lived there. In 1949, Kodo asked the abbot, Rev. Sokuo Eto, if his disciples could stay there and practice. Eventually Kodo took over Antaiji and became the fifth abbot, in name only—he continued to be a professor at Komazawa and travel throughout Japan to teach. He visited

Antaiji once a month to lead sesshins. His disciple Kosho Uchiyama started to live and practice there.

In March 1963, at the age of eighty-three, Kodo resigned from Komazawa. In June he stopped traveling due to his physical condition and retired to Antaiji. His moving monastery came to an end.

Kodo spent his final days at Antaiji. Kosho and his Dharma sister Rev. Joshin Kasai, together with a few younger monks, cared for Kodo until his death on December 21, 1965. Kosho held a forty-nine-day memorial sesshin in which the temple monks sat eight periods a day for forty-nine days. People who visited Antaiji to offer condolences were invited to sit zazen in front of Sawaki Roshi's relics. Kodo Sawaki Roshi left six male and ten female Dharma heirs.

Main Sources

Abe, Ryuichi, and Peter Haskel, trans. *Great Fool: Zen Master Ryokan.* Honolulu: University of Hawaii Press, 1996.

Bodhi, Bhikkhu, ed. *In the Buddha's Words: An Anthology of Discourses from the Pali Canon.* Boston: Wisdom Publications, 2005.

Jeffrey L. Broughton. *The Bodhidharma Anthology: The Earliest Records of Zen.* Berkeley: University of California Press, 1999.

The Buddhist Text Translation Society, Talmage, CA: Dharma Realm Buddhist University. Accessed online.

Clarke, John, trans. *Story of a Soul: The Autobiography of St. Therese of Lisieux.* 3rd ed. Washington, D.C.: ICS Publications, 1997.

Cleary, Thomas, trans. *Book of Serenity: One Hundred Zen Dialogues.* Hudson, NY: Lindisfarne Press, 1990.

Cook, Francis H., trans. *Demonstration of Consciousness Only: Three Texts on Consciousness Only.* Berkeley: Numara Center for Buddhist Translation and Research, 1999.

Ferguson, Andy. *Zen's Chinese Heritage: The Masters and their Teachings.* Boston: Wisdom Publications, 2000.

Heine, Steven. *The Zen Poetry of Dogen: Verses from the Mountain of Eternal Peace.* Mount Tremper, NY: Dharma Communications, 2005.

Hinton, David, trans. *The Analects.* Washington D.C.: Counterpoint, 1998.

Kato, Bunno, Yoshiro Tamura, and Kojiro Miyasaka, trans. *The Threefold Lotus Sutra.* Tokyo: Weatherhill, 1975.

Kaviratna, Harischandra, trans. *Dhammapada: Wisdom of the Buddha.* English-Pali Edition. Pasadena, CA: Theosophical University Press, 1989.

Leighton, Taigen Daniel, and Shohaku Okumura, trans. *Dogen's Pure Standards for the Zen Community: A Translation of Eihei Shingi.* Albany: State University of New York Press, 1996.

Nishijima, Gudo, and Chodo Cross, trans. *Master Dogen's Shobogenzo*, bk. 2. London: Windbell Publications, 1996.

Okumura, Shohaku, trans. *Heart of Zen: Practice Without Gaining-Mind.* Tokyo: Sotoshu Shumucho, 1988.

———. Shohaku, *Realizing Genjokoan*. Boston: Wisdom Publications, 2010.

———. Shohaku, trans. *Shobogenzo Zuimonki: Sayings of Eihei Dogen Zenji*. Tokyo: Sotoshu Shumucho, 1988.

Pascal, Blaise. *Pascal's Pensees*. New York: E.P. Dutton & Co., 1958.

Saddhatissa, H., trans. *The Sutta-Nipata*. Richmond: Curzon Press, 1985.

Sakai, Tokugen. *Sawaki Kodo Kikigaki: Life of a Zen Monk*. Tokyo: Kodansha, 1984.

Sawaki, Kodo. *Sawaki Kodo Zenshu.* 19 vols. Tokyo: Daihorinkaku, vol. 1, 1962.

Senauke, Hozan Alan. *The Bodhisattva's Embrace: Dispatches from Engaged Buddhism's Front Lines*. Berkeley: Clear View Press, 2010.

Suzuki, D. T. *Manual of Zen Buddhism*. New York: Grove Press, 1960.

———. *Zen and Japanese Culture*. Princeton: Princeton University Press, 1970.

Tanaka, Tadao. *Sawaki Kodo: Ancient Heart*. Tokyo: Daihorinkaku, 1990.

Tsunoda, Ryusaku, William Theodore De Bary, and Donald Keene, comps. *Sources of Japanese Tradition*, vol 1. New York: Columbia University Press, 1958.

Uchiyama, Kosho. *Jinseika Dokuhon* [Textbook for Human Life]. Tokyo: Hakujusha, 1980.

Unno, Taitetsu, trans. *Tannisho: A Shin Buddhist Classic*. Honolulu: Buddhist Study Center Press, 1984.

Victoria, Brian. *Zen at War.* New York: Weatherhill, 1997.

Walshe, Maurice, trans., *The Long Discourses of the Buddha: A Translation of the Digha Nikaya*. Boston: Wisdom Publications, 1995.

Yoshito, Hakeda. *Kukai: Major Works*. New York: Columbia University Press, 1972.

Index

how to live as the main concern of
  religion and education, 64–66
Huineng and Nanyue, 148q
human beings (people):
  aim (true aim), 197, 202–4
  attractiveness, 82–83
  as commodities in Japan, 33–34
  desires. *See* desires
  as ghosts, 77–78
  as idiots/foolish, 50, 82
  inertia, 67–68
  judging: by income, 113; standards
    for, 129
  living off organizations, 115–16
  lowest consciousness, 51
  making a living. *See* earning a living
  mistakes, 96–97
  nakedness, 72–73
  oneness with all beings, 178, 180
  as ordinary, 53
  tunnel vision, 52–54
  two groups (1% & 99%), 100
  views. *See* views
human life. *See under* life
human progress:
  material development vs., 18–20,
    40–41
  scientific advancement vs., 50–51,
    99–100

I
I, 169, 174, 175
  See also life force; the self
"...I am just who I am" (Uchiyama), 66
"I think, therefore I am," 175, 177
Ibaraki (town), 40–41
Ichida, Koshi, 2
identity (self-identity):
  loss of through group stupidity, 36
  self-definition by relationship/com-
    parison to others, 113, 217–18
  See also self
ideological notions of reality, 171

See also group stupidity
Ikeda, Eishin, 8
impermanence, 73, 116
  and interconnectedness, 180
  See also loss
income: judging someone's value by,
  113
inertia of human beings, 67–68
Inmo (Shobogenzo), 180q
"Instructions for the Cook" (Dogen),
  121+q, 166q, 183–84+q
intelligence and beyond, 162–63
intensity of practice, 140
interconnectedness:
  of all beings, 178, 180
  emptiness as, 175
  impermanence and, 180
  seeing the world from, 74–76
interdependent origination network,
  95, 100
intimacy with the Way/self:
  poverty and, 59
  zazen and, 25
Ishikawa Goemon, 22, 117–18
Ishimatsu, Mori no, 23
issaichi, 123

J
Japan:
  birthdays in, 142
  Buddhism as taught/not taught in,
    15, 16, 29, 150
  conditioning for war in, 47–48, 49
  educational system. *See* educational
    system of Japan
  fads in, 39–40
  group-oriented mentality, 36
  human beings as commodities in,
    33–34
  Meji period, 151
  military actions. *See* Japan's military
    actions
  as a money-making machine, 26

views:
of directions (lucky/unlucky), 87–88
fixed views, 150–51
habitual views, 168–70
of happiness, 31
of luck. *See* fortune or misfortune
superstitions, 88
tunnel vision, 52–54
women's views of men, 82–83, 113
See also false views
"A violet...as a violet...," 139, 140,
144–46
voluntary poverty, 59
vomiting the apple, 132, 133–34
vows:
bodhisattva vows, 32, 68, 181
to contribute to future generations,
95
vs. desires, 68

W
wabi-cha, 203
wandering within samsara, 108
war:
conditioning for in Japan, 47–48, 49
Sawaki Roshi's comments on, 5, 47,
84, 104; Okumura on, 5–7
See also Japan's military actions
waste, 204
water: fights over, 74, 75
the Way (buddha way):
as empty and clear, 75
intimacy with the Way/self, 25, 59
the path beyond loss and gain, 101–3
studying: as studying the self, 25–26,
66, 162–63, 212. *See also* studying
the self
toddling/stumbling/limping along
the path, 122–24
See also reality
wealth:
attractiveness of, 82
impermanence (family losses), 73, 83

"What am I going to do?" dance,
199–201
"What is life?" question (Uchiyama),
210–11
"Whatever happens, I am I," 122
"whichever, whatever, wherever"
attitude, 227
Whitehead, Jokei Molly Delight, 3, 260
preface to this book, xiii–xiv
Whyte, William H.: *The Organization
Man*, 36
wisdom:
all knowing, 123
of the five aggregates, 198
four kinds, 109
women: views of men, 82–83, 113
working. *See* earning a living
world:
religious vs. secular, 197
seeing as the content of zazen, 74–76,
188–89
worldly life as like scrambling for
clouds, 224
"...a worm in the rice," 204
worship of a teacher, 125–26
Wu, Emperor, and Bodhidharma, 112

X
"Xinxinming" (Sengcan), 75q, 153q
Xuanzang, 169
Xuedou, 166q

Y
Yadonashi Hokku-san, 14
Yamada, Reirin, 16q
Yangshan and Guishan, 149q
Yaoshan, 124q
Yogacara:
Consciousness Only teaching, 108–9,
169–70+q, 172–73+q
Kodo's studies of, 238, 239
Sawaki Roshi's teachings on, 168,
169+q, 174

About the Authors

 **Kosho Uchiyama** was born in Tokyo in 1912. He received a master's degree in Western philosophy at Waseda University in 1937 and became a Zen priest three years later under Kodo Sawaki Roshi. Upon Sawaki's death in 1965, he became abbot of Antaiji, a temple and monastery then located on the outskirts of Kyoto. Uchiyama Roshi developed the practice at Antaiji and ordained more than twenty people. He retired from Antaiji in 1975 and lived with his wife at Nokein, a small temple outside Kyoto, where he continued to write, publish, and meet with the many people who found their way to his door, until his death in 1998. He wrote over twenty books on Zen, including translations of Dogen Zenji in modern Japanese with commentaries, as well as various shorter essays. His *Opening the Hand of Thought: Foundations of Zen Buddhist Practice* is available in English from Wisdom Publications. He was an origami master as well as a Zen master and published several books on origami.

 **Shohaku Okumura** is a Soto Zen priest and Dharma successor of Kosho Uchiyama Roshi. He is a graduate of Komazawa University and has practiced in Japan at Antaiji, Zuioji, and the Kyoto Soto Zen Center, and in Massachusetts at the Pioneer Valley Zendo. He is the former director of the Soto Zen Buddhism International Center in San Francisco. His previously published books of translation include Uchiyama Roshi's *Opening the Hand of Thought*, as well as *Dogen's Extensive Record: A Translation of the Eihei Koroku*, with Taigen Dan Leighton. He is the author of *Living by Vow: A Practical Introduction to Eight Essential Zen Chants and Texts* and *Realizing Genjokoan: The Key to Dogen's Shobogenzo*. He is the founding teacher of the Sanshin Zen Community, based in Bloomington, Indiana, where he lives with his family.

 **Jokei Molly Delight Whitehead** studied comparative literature at Harvard University before working as a writer, newspaper editor, and teacher. Her practice began at Tassajara Zen Mountain Center in 1997. She then lived in Japan for five years, teaching English and visiting as many temples as possible. She began studying with Shohaku Okumura in 2007 and was ordained in 2011. These days, she writes a blog at polishingthemoon.com and sits Antaiji-style sesshins in the tradition of her lineage.

Living by Vow
A Practical Introduction to Eight Essential Zen Chants and Texts
Shohaku Okumura

"An essential resource for students and teachers alike."
—Dosho Port, author of *Keep Me in Your Heart a While*

Making Zen Your Own
Giving Life to Twelve Key Golden Age Ancestors
Janet Jiryu Abels

"Abels's rich and succinct descriptions of the lives of the Zen ancestors will help many find their own way into the Zen path."
—Andy Ferguson, author of *Zen's Chinese Heritage*

Opening the Hand of Thought
Foundations of Zen Buddhist Practice
Kosho Uchiyama

"If you read one book on Zen this year, this should be that book."
—James Ishmael Ford, head teacher of Boundless Way Zen and author of *If You're Lucky, Your Heart Will Break*

Realizing Genjokoan
The Key to Dogen's Shobogenzo
Shohaku Okumura

"A stunning commentary. Like all masterful commentaries, this one finds in the few short lines of the text the entire span of the Buddhist teachings."
—*Buddhadharma: The Buddhist Review*

Zen Questions
Zazen, Dogen, and the Spirit of Creative Inquiry
Taigen Dan Leighton

"Taigen Dan Leighton's clear, accurate, and eminently useful book
will save any serious Zen practitioner, or even a curious novice,
years of wasted error, wrong turns, and plain old delusion."
—Peter Coyote

Deepest Practice, Deepest Wisdom
Three Fascicles from Shobogenzo with Commentary
Kosho Uchiyama
Translated by Shohaku Okumura and Tom Wright

"Real Dharma. The mingled voices of these teachers—inspiring,
challenging, sage, and earthy—shake dust from the mind so we may
see more clearly what's right here."—Ben Connelly, author of *Inside
Vasubandhu's Yogacara: A Practitioner's Guide*

About Wisdom Publications

Wisdom Publications is the leading publisher of classic and contemporary Buddhist books and practical works on mindfulness. To learn more about us or to explore our other books, please visit our website at wisdomexperience.org or contact us at the address below.

Wisdom Publications
199 Elm Street
Somerville, MA 02144 USA

We are a 501(c)(3) organization, and donations in support of our mission are tax deductible.

Wisdom Publications is affiliated with the Foundation for the Preservation of the Mahayana Tradition (FPMT).